THE SAVVINESS TO UNDERSTANDING
AND EMBRACING THE SABBATH

THE SAVVINESS TO UNDERSTANDING AND EMBRACING THE SABBATH

A Journey from Sunday to Saturday

BY LAWRENCE A. SAUNDERS, M.TH. AND JUNE TYSON, PhD

XULON PRESS ELITE

Xulon Press Elite
2301 Lucien Way #415
Maitland, FL 32751
407.339.4217
www.xulonpress.com

Printed in the United States of America.

Paperback ISBN-13: 978-1-5456-7843-5
eBook ISBN-13: 978-1-5456-7844-2

Acknowledgments xi

We Have a Testimony xiii

Introduction xxv

Section 1: Laying the Sabbath Foundation 1

  1. The Creation of Rest 3

  2. Jehovah God, The First to Keep the Sabbath 5

  3. The Sabbath is the Only Day God Named 8

  4. The Dynamics of the Forth Commandment 10

  5. The Sabbath, A Universal Principle 12

  6. Sabbath Then, Sabbath Now, Sabbath Forever 14

  7. Not the sabbath(s), but THE Sabbath 17

  8. The Sabbath is a Day for Rest, Not Wrest 18

  9. Jesus Kept the Sabbath; Jesus is Lord of
      the Sabbath 20

10. Observing the Sabbath, One of the Greatest
      Sacrifices 22

11. From Sacrifice to Sublimity 23

12. For God So Loved the World, He Gave Us
      the Sabbath 27

13. Who Else Kept the Sabbath? 28

14. There Was More Than One Law 30

15. Do You Practice "Ceremonial-ism?" 35

16. Worship God, Not the Sabbath 39

**Section 2: A Historical Overview of the Evolution of
the Sabbath** 41

17. The Consequences of Constantine 43

18. Tradition Verses Truth. 45

19. Man Changed the Times, Not God 47

20. Why the Devil Doesn't Want Us To Keep
the Sabbath 54

21. The Difference Between the Sabbath and Every
Other Weekday 56

22. The Strongest Proof in the New Testament For
Keeping the Sabbath Today 59

23. Although Jesus Gives Us Rest, We Still Have to Keep
the Sabbath 70

24. Keep the Sabbath Because of Love, Not Law 73

25. Sabbath, Not Sadness 75

26. So What? Jesus Didn't Say It; He Did It 77

27. Stop Working On The Sabbath 79

28. Why Not Still Observe the Sabbath? 81

Section 3: Life in the Lord of the Sabbath 83

29. The Sabbath, The Holiest Day of Them
All, PERIOD 85

30. The Sabbath is not Just a DAY; it is a WAY 87

31. What Does God Say We Should Not Do During the
Sabbath? 90

32. How to Keep JESUS in the Sabbath 94

33. Eight Benefits of Observing the Sabbath 101

34. Keeping the Sabbath Can Enhance Our
    Relationships............................ 107
35. Effective Ways to Use Your Time During
    the Sabbath 111
36. Activities To Do on the Sabbath 115
37. Which Do You Love More, The Sign or
    the Savior? 117
38. The Fulfillment of Observing the Sabbath, Oneness
    with God 119
39. Sharing this Information 121
40. Sabbath Observance, From Revelation to
    Revolution............................... 128

Conclusion: The Salvation Message...................131
References...................................... 133
About the Book 135
About the Authors 137

This Book is Dedicated To

The Past
John and Elizabeth McKinney, our great grandparents, who
left us a legacy of freedom and hard work.

The Present
Our parents, George and Shirley Saunders,
Greely and Halestine Tyson, for teaching us the importance
of love and family loyalty.

The Future
Lawrence Saunders II and Rachel Grace Pettway, to whom
we are "passing the torch," to perpetuate the light of our
family legacy of loving and serving the Lord Jesus Christ.

Acknowledgments

*W*e would like to thank our Lord and Savior, Jesus Christ, whose Holy Spirit guided us every step of the way in writing this book.

Thank you, Pastor John Millwood and First Lady Michelle, for reinforcing the relevance of keeping the Sabbath today.

Thank you, Elders Robert McDonald and Sharon Grier, for patiently taking time with us in the beginning of our journey to ignite a desire to delve deeper into the truth regarding the Sabbath.

Thank you, Lawrence Saunders II, for giving us the gift of your critical thinking by asking questions and adding pertinent information that helped us express our message in a manner that is comprehensive and applicable.

We would like to give a special acknowledgment to Supreme Court Justice Genine D. Edwards. Thank you for allowing God to use you to introduce us to the Sabbath. For more than 20 years, you have been a consistent witness, who shared your faith in Jesus Christ and your belief in the importance of the Sabbath for believers today. You have profoundly affected our lives in a tremendous way. We are grateful to God for your commitment to the truth. We praise the Lord that you did not give up on us.

Special Note of Thanks

We would like to thank the following people who assisted us in our formative years. God used their gifts and ministry to help make us the servants of God we are today. Thank you for remaining true to your calling.

Bishop Wilbert Mckinnely
Bishop Gerald G. Seabrooks
Bishop Marvin L. Winans
Bishop H. Curtis Douglas
Pastor Flora Grant
Pastor A. R. Bernard
Fred Hammond
The Winans
Commissioned

We Have a Testimony

*L*awrence Saunders Sr. and June Tyson are cousins who grew up in Brooklyn, New York, in a fun-loving family, who enjoyed coming together and celebrating life. They attended church at times, and it was always an enjoyable experience; however, they were not "born again," so going to church did not have any significant meaning until 1982.

In 1982, Lawrence's eldest brother, Eric Saunders Sr., passed away at the age of 24, leaving a void in Lawrence's life. It was his brother's death that brought Lawrence to a place of utter brokenness.

Lawrence was in high school and had no true knowledge of Jesus. As a means of coping with the intense pain he was enduring, this 17-year-old young man turned heavily to drinking alcohol to try to escape his "hurting reality."

During a most unlikely encounter from a most unlikely source, however, he came to receive Jesus as Lord of his life. There was a person in Lawrence's class that he was sorely afraid of. This young man had red eyes and a dark complexion, but his character was the darkest part of him. To Lawrence, he was the "meanest person on earth" and "a bully of bullies." He was respected by many but feared by all. He had fights every day. This prompted Lawrence to give him a nickname, "The Black Cat," because of his ruthless ways.

Lawrence and quite a few others would do everything in their power to stay out of the path of "The Black Cat," so going to school was not an enjoyable experience. Lawrence was happy to go on the winter recess because he wanted a break from school, but more so from "The Black Cat." Unfortunately, it turned out to be the worst recess from school he would ever encounter.

It was during this time when Lawrence's brother, Eric, passed away, and his life seemed to spiral out of control. He began relying on alcohol daily to help him endure his loss. But upon returning to school after recess, he noticed a remarkable and drastic change in the life of "The Black Cat."

His countenance was so much lighter, as his face had a radiant glow to it. His once-bloodshot eyes were now white and clear. He also went from wearing jeans and sneakers every day to wearing suits, ties, and dress shoes. Best of all, he stopped fighting, which was his trademark. Instead he started training as a boxer and practiced his craft often.

When Lawrence saw this seemingly instantaneous transformation, he was curious as to what caused it. So, one day, after getting up the courage, Lawrence reluctantly approached him and told him he noticed a tremendous change in him. He asked him, "Why are you so quiet and not fighting anymore?" He informed Lawrence that during the recess, he went to church and surrendered his life to Christ.

"The Black Cat" then gave Lawrence 2 Corinthians 5:17 (KJV), which says, "Therefore if any man [be] in Christ, [he is] a new creature: old things are passed away; behold, all things are become new." After hearing that scripture, Lawrence felt something move inside him. He was truly mesmerized and could not believe the enormous change he saw in "The Black Cat." Lawrence recalled thinking, *Wow, if Jesus could help change "The Black Cat," then maybe Jesus could change my life as well.*

"The Black Cat" invited Lawrence to attend a Friday night service at his church in Brooklyn. Lawrence did not make that service, but he did go the following Sunday. Despite hearing the church's evangelist preach a compelling sermon, Lawrence did not heed to the altar appeal to receive Christ.

It was not until the service was over that Lawrence was invited into the Fellowship Hall where he met the preacher, who said to Lawrence, "I can tell you are going through much pain right now." Lawrence told her she was correct because his brother had recently passed away. Her response to him was, "If you receive Jesus into your heart, He will take your great pain away."

Lawrence, who was desperately seeking relief, began to reflect on where his life was headed. He thought about how his abuse of alcohol had so many devastating effects, not only on him, but on so many people he loved. After pondering that thought, Lawrence accepted Jesus Christ into his life on

October 21, 1982. This began Lawrence's personal, "Genesis." His life would never be the same, as he has been in a loving relationship with Christ ever since.

Meanwhile, June, also a teenager, was experiencing some serious growing pains. In 1986, at the age of 18, Lawrence shared with June a Gospel tape by The Winans. God used the words of that music to touch every growing pain she was suffering from.

June knew she wanted to live for Jesus, especially after seeing the change He had made in the life of her cousin, Lawrence. After months of thinking deeply about her life and the problems she was experiencing at that time, she decided to give her life to God. On Sunday, January 19, 1986, June went to a friend's church, intending to give her life to the Lord. She was saved and baptized that day.

June grew in her walk with the Lord by immersing herself in the Word of God, participating in the choir, and attending Bible study and prayer consistently. In addition, Lawrence took her to church, Bible school, tent meetings, concerts, revivals, and fellowships, and they would often meet to study the Word of God at her home.

In the meantime, Lawrence was so overwhelmed at the difference in his life after Jesus had become his Lord and Savior that he felt compelled to give back to God for all He had done for him. So Lawrence enrolled in a Bible school to learn more about God, as he felt it would increase his ability to serve Him, and he joined an Apostolic church that was built upon a foundation of prayer and holiness and served in various capacities there. Lawrence was an usher, a Sunday school teacher, and a singer in the choir. As he grew closer to God, Lawrence felt the call to preach the gospel, and in 1985, he became an ordained minister.

After serving faithfully at the first church he attended, in 1991, he was led by the Lord to join a Fire Baptized Holiness Church. It was at this church that Lawrence really began to flourish in his growth and development as a man of God. He was introduced to the concept of worship, and he was taught how to study and exegete scripture like he never had been. Lawrence was also a worship leader at this church, an adult Sunday school teacher, an associate pastor, and finally a youth pastor.

Lawrence truly enjoyed serving God and His people and was inspired by his pastor to attend Bible college. After graduation, he went to seminary, where he earned a Master's degree in Theology. He had a profound love for studying God and His word, an attribute instilled in him by his former pastor and mentor from the Fire Baptized Holiness Church where he was serving.

During this time, in 1994, June became disenchanted with the church as a whole. She believed the church should have been doing more work to serve the hurting masses in the community, and she was not seeing enough of this from the church of Jesus Christ.

So, she began to isolate herself from Lawrence and her family because she knew they would try to persuade her not to leave the church. She began to explore the religion of Al-Islam, but Jesus would not let her go that easily, and she quickly began to see that Al-Islam did not have the same impact as Jesus' work on the cross, something June depended on greatly for her eternal destiny. It didn't take long before June realized from deeply painful experiences that Jesus is truly "The Way, The Truth, and The Life." So after three years of being out of fellowship with Jesus, she rededicated her life to the Lord.

Lawrence and June reconnected after she returned to the church. They began to pray together about their personal lives and the state of their family. It became especially important to them that their family knew the joy of life in Christ and the security of having everlasting life. At this point, they connected with two other born-again Christian members of their family and committed to asking God to hold back the winds of destruction from them, as stated in Revelation 7:1 (BSB): "After this I saw four angels standing at the four corners of the earth, holding back its four winds so that no wind would blow on land or sea or on any tree." In fact, they used this scripture to name their ministry "Holding Back the Winds," which was dedicated to praying for their unsaved family members. They also held fellowships where they gathered with their Christian friends to share the Word and a good meal.

In 1999, Lawrence was led by God to join Christian Life Center, which soon became Christian Cultural Center (CCC), in Brooklyn. Lawrence felt his experience there was desperately needed. At CCC, he learned the essence of teaching the Word of God and not just preaching it. He also learned structure, one of the greatest assets he could have acquired.

At CCC, Lawrence saw and experienced what a structured church service and ministry was all about. Lawrence was blown away by the order of the service and the way the church functioned. It was on a level and in a manner he had never seen before in a church setting. After learning so much from his church and ministry experiences, Lawrence was about to find out why the Lord had placed him in each church he belonged to at the appropriate times.

Establishing a Church

As the Lord would have it, in 2002, out of a love for praying and for imparting knowledge of the Word of God to others, Lawrence began to have prayer and Bible study meetings at his apartment every Wednesday night. At first, they had only a few attendees. After only three months, however, the attendance began to blossom.

In the meantime, Lawrence felt the call of God to plant a church. At first, he wrestled with the thought, as he did not feel he could handle the responsibility of such an enormous calling. But after truly seeking the Lord, he heard clearly and received numerous confirmations from a variety of sources that the Lord had chosen him to pastor the church.

So, Lawrence informed those who attended the weekly Bible study what he felt the Lord had called him to do, and they were all on board with it. His cousin, June, was his right-hand person in the planning phases of the ministry. At first, he named the church The Living Room Life Ministry because they were having services in his living room. But after further praying about the name, the Lord instructed him to name the church Word For Life Christian Center. In five months, by the Lord's divine hand, Lawrence was miraculously able to secure a building where the church services would be held. On May 5, 2002, Word For Life Christian Center had its first official Sunday worship service. Since then, Word for Life Christian Center has served the community of Bedford-Stuyvesant in Brooklyn for nearly two decades, with fidelity and commitment. Many souls have come to accept Jesus Christ as their Lord and Savior.

Our Journey to the Sabbath

The first time Lawrence heard about the relevance and necessity of keeping the Sabbath was not in a church. It was brought to his attention by a longtime friend of more than 20 years, who once faithfully attended a Sunday church before adhering to the seventh-day Saturday Sabbath. She was extremely excited about embracing the Sabbath and would often share knowledge about her newfound experience with Lawrence.

At this time, Lawrence was still the Senior Pastor of Word For Life Christian Center. He would listen to what his friend had to say about the Sabbath, and the two would often have lengthy discussions about it. During that time, Lawrence believed honoring the Sabbath was no longer needed for today's church. He erroneously thought the requirement for keeping the Sabbath was "under the law." In fact, he would strongly debate with her about that point and would not relent. His friend, however, was patient, committed, and faithful to her belief about the Sabbath. So, they came to a respectable impasse while remaining distant friends, all the while continuing to talk about it for nearly twenty years.

But on December 2, 2017, Lawrence connected with her, and they began a more consistent and purposeful dialogue about the Sabbath. While Lawrence still refused to accept what she had to say about the Sabbath, he visited her church, which was a Seventh Day Adventist (SDA) Church. His friend invited him to a variety of services and community events and he attended them. She also gave him books and invited him to read the SDA quarterly, which was composed of daily Bible lessons.

All these things ignited a spark in Lawrence, but it was not to embrace the Sabbath. On the contrary, he intensively studied the Bible and various sources and commentaries, seeking to totally dispel her claim that God still requires His church to keep the Fourth Commandment today, which is to "Remember the Sabbath day, to keep it holy." (Exodus 20:8, KJV)

One of the first people Lawrence reached out to was his cousin, June, whom he considered to be a knowledgeable source of the Bible, particularly when it came to understanding the Old Testament. He had relied on her Old Testament knowledge for many years. After contacting June, she quickly jumped on board with helping Lawrence disprove the relevance for today's church to still keep the Sabbath. But after about three weeks of intrinsic research, study, and investigation, something oddly wonderful happened.

After Lawrence contacted June to discuss what she learned regarding the Sabbath, neither of them found any scriptural evidence that convinced them that keeping the Sabbath was no longer required by God. In fact, they agreed that it was, and still is, God's desire and eternal commandment that everyone continue to "Remember the Sabbath to keep it holy." This was a profound revelation for both of them. So they wasted no time in committing themselves fully to learning about and keeping the Sabbath.

Today, they often acquaint their journey along this road to embracing the Sabbath to the Apostle Paul's journey on his road to accepting Christianity. Before his conversion, Paul, who was then known as Saul, had his heart set on disproving everything about Christianity and destroying the church as he "made havock, of the church," as stated in Acts 8:3 (KJV). But the Lord changed his name and, more importantly, his heart, and he became a Christian instead of persecuting Christians.

Both Lawrence and June could relate to Paul, as the Lord also gave them a great change of heart, and they went from discrediting the necessity of the Sabbath to fully living and loving it. Only the Lord Himself could turn the hearts of two Christians, who, for more than thirty years each, enjoyed going to church on Sunday without any problem at all. It was all they knew. They both praise God for revealing His truth about the Sabbath to them; as a result, they are experiencing a whole new level of blessings from Him.

The Enlightening

After more than thirty years of attending and holding church services on Sunday, holding primary worship services on Saturday was a bit of a culture shock for Lawrence and June. They had a combined seventy years of experience of attending church services on Sunday. In all those years, June had heard only one sermon about honoring the Sabbath, and Lawrence hadn't heard any. So they had no experience to assist them in practicing the Sabbath. But after embracing the Sabbath, they were anxious to learn how to practice it and how to prepare for it so they could be sure to observe it properly.

So, during their first week of observing the Sabbath, Lawrence and June asked various people questions, but were not satisfied with the answers they received. They knew they needed the "milk of the Word," as it pertained to the Sabbath because they were young in Sabbath observance and needed to grow. The people they were asking, however, were not even giving them "milk." While these people understood the "letter" of Sabbath observance, Lawrence and June were looking for the "Spirit" of the practice. They were, therefore, left in confusion.

So, Lawrence arranged for a brother and two sisters, who were ardent Seventh Day Adventists, to talk to him and June about Sabbath observance. But because they were aware of their extensive church experience, they tailored the lessons accordingly. Lawrence and June still needed more basic information about understanding and growing in the Sabbath.

At this point, the Holy Spirit began to teach Lawrence and June how to observe the Sabbath His way, by giving them new revelations they were not receiving from anyone else. He knew they were hungry to know how to practice the Sabbath in a way that would give God glory and build a closer relationship with Him. So, He taught them Himself, beginning with Proverbs 4:18 (KJV): "The path of the just is as a shining light, that shineth more and more unto the perfect day." This scripture describes the daily experience of someone during the first month of Sabbath keeping.

The Holy Spirit's Work

Lawrence and June discussed writing an article about their experience of transitioning from Sundays as their primary day for attending worship services, to Saturdays. Suddenly, the conversation moved from writing an article to writing a book. Once this decision was made, Lawrence and June began writing profusely and freely.

As they began rereading what they were writing, they were amazed because what they had written sounded nothing like them. The ideas and concepts were profound and wise, far above the intelligence of Lawrence and June. So they had no other recourse than to conclude the writing was being done by the Holy Spirit Himself. It was then they prayed He would take full control of this work and make it His own. Since then they have maintained this prayer with diligence and consistency. This book is the result of their prayers.

Introduction

*O*ur journey to honoring the Sabbath was a strange one. We were on a mission to "Sabotage the Sabbath." We were both studying information about the Sabbath, with the intention of disproving its relevance in the life of today's Christian. We were under the misconception that the Fourth Commandment was part of the Ceremonial Law and therefore abolished by the work of Jesus on the cross. In light of our research, however, the Lord revealed to us that adhering to the Sabbath is crucial to one's spiritual life. It was significant before the Moral and Mosaic Law, after Jesus' resurrection, and remains relevant for everyone to observe today.

If you are reading this book, we believe God has a wonderful blessing in store for you. We have been encouraged by the Lord to share information that has changed our lives significantly. Before honoring the Sabbath, we were both stagnated in our salvation experience. We were not thriving or doing work for God that was reviving or particularly stimulating. After hearing the clear voice of the Lord regarding embracing the Sabbath, however, we felt as though a fresh anointing was imparted upon us. It was as if we had been born again...again.

Although you will hear us often refer to terms that make reference to the Ten Commandments, particularly the Sabbath, and both the Moral Law and the Ceremonial Mosaic Covenant, none of these have the ability to save us from sin. Only Jesus saves. Matthew 1:21 (KJV) says, "And she shall bring forth a son, and thou shalt call his name JESUS: for he shall save his people from their sins." Peter solidifies this point by making this profound declaration in Acts 4:12 (KJV): "Neither is there salvation in any other: for there is none other name under heaven given among men, whereby we must be saved." We appreciate how the Contemporary English Version (CEV) puts it: "Only Jesus has the power to save! His name is the only one in all the world that can save anyone."

We are not placing the Sabbath or the Moral and Ceremonial Law above being born again by receiving Jesus Christ as Lord and Savior. No one can truly keep the Sabbath without first being in a covenant relationship with Jesus, who is Lord of the Sabbath according to Matthew 12:8 (KJV): "For the Son of man is Lord even of the Sabbath day."

In this statement, Jesus is making the point that He is much greater than the Sabbath. Look at the exact words He uses: "For the Son of man [Jesus Himself] is Lord." Then He uses the word *even* in "even of the Sabbath day" to let His audience, the Pharisees and us, know the importance of keeping the Sabbath, as He is Lord of it. The word *Lord* in the Greek means "the commander, ruler, superintendent, and controller over and above everyone, everything, and every day, including the Sabbath day." So, please, keep this concept in mind as you read this book.

As much as the Law is powerful, wonderful, and needed, it did not have the ability to save anyone from the penalty of sin, which is death. Only Jesus can do this. Romans 6:23 (KJV) says, "For the wages of sin [is] death; but the gift of God [is] eternal life through Jesus Christ our Lord."

This is exactly why God had to send Jesus to die for our sins. Romans 8:3 (KJV) says, "For what the law could not do, in that it was weak through the flesh, God sending his own Son in the likeness of sinful flesh, and for sin, condemned sin in the flesh." The Amplified version makes this point stand out:

> For what the Law could not do [that is, over-
> come sin and remove its penalty, its power]
> being weakened by the flesh [man's nature
> without the Holy Spirit], God did: He sent His
> own Son in the likeness of sinful man as an
> offering for sin. And He condemned sin in the
> flesh [subdued it and overcame it in the person
> of His own Son].

The Law was only a "shadow," but Christ is the reality and finality to completely save us and secure our salvation. Hebrews 10:1 (NKJV) says, "For the law, having a shadow of the good things to come, [and] not the very image of the things, can never with these same sacrifices, which they offer

continually year by year, make those who approach perfect."
The New English Translation (NET) says is this way: "For the
law possesses a shadow of the good things to come but not the
reality itself, and is therefore completely unable, by the same
sacrifices offered continually, year after year, to perfect those
who come to worship."

Hebrews 7:19 (KJV) says, "For the law made nothing perfect: on the other hand, there is the bringing in of a better hope,
through which we draw nigh unto God." This is why God, out
of His love for us, sent Jesus, "...His only begotten Son," our
"Blessed Hope," even before the world or time existed ("from
the foundation of the world," Revelation 13:8, KJV), to fulfill
God's requirement and demand to fully pay the penalty of our
sin and rescue us from the "wages of sin, death."

It is our sincere prayer and desire that those who read this
book who are not saved (born-again believers), and have not
invited Jesus to be Lord of their lives, would do so. We also pray
that those who accepted Christ but do not embrace the Sabbath
by "Remembering to keep it holy" would seriously open their
hearts and minds to make the decision to agree with this biblically based truth. This our prayer. In Jesus' name, Amen.

The Goal (Proof, Not Prove)

We did not write this book to try to *prove* the Sabbath is
God's will for His children (us) to observe. Just by the mere
fact that God spoke it and it is written in His Word proves to
us that He wants us all to "Remember the Sabbath, by keeping

it holy," (NIV). We did write this book, however, to show the *proof*, evidence, and facts that the mandate for us to keep the Sabbath still stands and is something that all His children, "the people of God," must still keep today.

Anyone who truly believes the entire Bible is God's infallible word should also believe in and embrace keeping the Sabbath. We are sure you have heard the old expressions, "If God said it, I believe it," and "God said it, I believe it, and that settles it." But how can this be if you are not obeying Him when He clearly tells us to "Remember the Sabbath by keeping it holy"? If you are not doing this, you must ask yourself, "Why?" Please think about this point as you read this book. We are sure you will get a clearer understanding about the Sabbath.

The goal of this book is not to convince you to observe the Sabbath, or to persuade you to adhere to the teachings of a specific religious group, affiliation, denomination, or reformation. It is not our goal to encourage you to stop attending worship services on Sundays. We are not of any denomination. We are simply Seventh-Day Sabbath-observing Christians who love Jesus.

Our primary goal is to lift up the name of Jesus and point you in the direction of the cross in all we say in this book. You will find that Jesus is the center of every section of our writing. In pointing people to Jesus, we also want to eliminate the complexities of sharing the undeniable truth about the Sabbath, to help people observe the Sabbath, and to receive the benefits and blessings thereof.

The Title... What's It All About?

Allow us to explain the meaning of the title of this book, *The Savviness to Understanding and Embracing the Sabbath.* The word *savvy* is defined as, "experienced, knowledgeable, well-informed, and shrewd." It also means "having a practical understanding; or intelligence; common sense, to know; or understand."

The goal of this book is to help people become more experienced, knowledgeable, and well-informed about the importance of keeping the Sabbath. In illustrating this goal, there are two imperative factors we want to expound upon:

1. To explain what observing the Sabbath means.

2. To explain why it is relevant for us, God's creation, to continue to observe the Sabbath, even today.

Section 1

Laying the Sabbath Foundations

In this section, we will establish the Sabbath as a fundamental, foundational truth that was part of the creation of the world. We will show it is an institution and part of the lives of early man. Finally, we will demonstrate the Sabbath is an unending desire of God for all of us to have a deeper and meaningful relationship with Him.

1

The Creation of Rest

*M*any believe creation took place in six days, which is true in terms of God's creative tangible activities. The Lord created one intangible act, however, on the seventh day: the principle of rest (the Sabbath). Yes, rest was something God actually created. Creation, therefore, took place in seven days, and on the seventh day, God created rest, which allowed Him to admire everything He had made the previous six days. Rest, therefore, was the finality of God's creation. In creating it, this day (the Sabbath) became holy, different, and unlike any of the other six days. At that point, the seven-day week was established permanently in time. Because of this, the inspiration of rest is perpetuated every seventh day of the week.

If we are sensitive to the Holy Spirit, we can sense there is an element of sanctification and sublime blessedness in the atmosphere every seventh day of the week (the Sabbath).

Considering the hallowedness of the day, we are to make time to rest as God did, to appreciate creation and all it entails. When we do this, we must do it fully, by completely abstaining from all of life's common daily self-pleasures. Resting on the Sabbath leads to a greater reverence not only for who God is, but also for what He has done and is still doing for us. A fuller comprehension of the Lord Jesus, who He is and what He means to us, can be seen when we truly stop and rest, just as Moses told the children of Israel to do in Exodus 14:13 (KJV), "Stand still and see the salvation of the Lord."

The Lord also instructs us in Psalm 46:10 (KJV) to "Be still and know that I am God." This text further proves we can truly observe and recognize God with much greater understanding by "being still," which means to be in a state of rest. There is no way we can absorb anything close to the magnitude the of Lord's creativity and, more importantly, the overall majesty of who He is in all His true splendor if we are distracted by the cares and obligations of this world. We must, therefore, be in a position of mental, physical, and spiritual rest to absolutely "Keep the Sabbath day holy." So, reader, we encourage you to rest. God created it, He did it, that settles it, so let's do it.

2

Jehovah God, The First to Keep the Sabbath

he two crucial points we want to share with you in this section are:

1. God was the first to keep the Sabbath.

2. Keeping the Sabbath is still relevant and important for us to do today.

When God created the earth, He rested on the Sabbath day and made it "holy," different and distinct from all the other days. We find it to be truly remarkable that God, the One who has unlimited power and never gets tired, took time off from His business of creation to rest. God was the first to keep the Sabbath. This shows the glory and the vitality of this special day. We see this clearly in Genesis 2:1-3 (KJV):

> Thus the heavens and the earth were completed
> in all their vast array. By the seventh day God
> had finished the work he had been doing; so, on
> the seventh day (the Sabbath) he rested from all
> his work. Then God blessed the seventh day and
> made it holy, because on it he rested from all the
> work of creating that he had done.

If God kept the Sabbath, what makes us believe we should not? It is a day unlike any other day of the week. God treated this day differently by doing something different: He rested.

The Lord also attested to the unending fact that the Sabbath is an everlasting agreement for all creation to observe throughout eternity. In Exodus 31:16 (KJV), He says, "Wherefore the children of Israel shall keep the Sabbath, to observe the Sabbath throughout their generations, for a perpetual covenant." God says that we (spiritual Israel via our relationship by faith through Abraham) shall keep the Sabbath "throughout our generations, for a perpetual covenant." This means it is a never-ending contract that the Lord gave all of us to recognize and keep. We believe, just as God does, that resting is essential for us to have the spiritual, physical, emotional, and mental strength, not only to live, but to do all the Lord has called us to do.

In an article entitled, "How to Bring a Spirit of Sabbath Into Your Daily Life," Pastian (2019), makes a fascinating statement that captures the essence and reflects the wonderful benefits that come about as a result of taking a Sabbath rest. He said:

The idea of resting could be a lost art. And when I say 'resting' I am not talking about Netflix bingeing. Rest comes in many forms, but the best kind of rest is one that rejuvenates the body, soul, and spirit. It rekindles a fire in you again. A Sabbath is unique because it is a God-initiated and God-inspired rest that replenishes holistically. I do not think this kind of rest has to be so complicated and so difficult to find. Being encouraged to rest at the right times might be the best leadership advice you could ever receive.

3

The Sabbath is the Only
Day God Named

$\mathcal{A}$nother distinction regarding the Sabbath is that it's the only day God named. The other six days of the week were named by man, but the Lord called the seventh day "the Sabbath." The word *Sabbath* is first seen in Exodus 16:23 (NIV): "He said to them, 'This is what the LORD commanded: "Tomorrow is to be a day of Sabbath rest, a holy Sabbath to the LORD. So, bake what you want to bake and boil what you want to boil. Save whatever is left and keep it until morning."'"

After this point, the seventh day is referred to as "the Sabbath." The only other identifiable day of the week in Scripture is "the first day of the week," a phrase used eight times in the King James Version: Matthew 28:1; Mark 16:2,9; Luke 24:1; John 20:1,19; Acts 20:7; and 1 Corinthians 16:2.

God is showing us that naming this distinct day makes the Sabbath very special and worthy of serious consideration and reflection. Let us do this by learning more about it in greater detail in the Fourth Commandment.

4

The Dynamics of the Forth Commandment

The Fourth Commandment is noticeably different from the other nine Commandments in five ways:

1. It is the longest of the Ten Commandments, consisting of four verses with detailed information on how to keep this Commandment.

2. All the other Commandments address relationship, but the Fourth Commandment focuses on the importance of a day and "keeping it holy."

3. In this Commandment, we see the order of creation. Exodus 20:11 (KJV) states, "For in six days the LORD made the heavens and the earth, the sea, and all that is in them, but he rested on the seventh day. Therefore, the LORD blessed the Sabbath day and made it holy."

4. It is the only Commandment out of all the other nine that God specifically says must be "kept throughout all generations as a perpetual covenant," meaning there is no end to us keeping the Sabbath.

5. The Fourth Commandment depicts the aspects of a specific day. This day should be celebrated and enjoyed by all mankind, not just Christians and Jews. In fact, we believe it once was.

5

The Sabbath, A
Universal Principle

The principle of the Sabbath was given, practiced, cherished, and respected by mankind before the end of the first week of creation, before the Law was given in Exodus 16:23-29. In fact, more than 100 different languages have named their seventh day of the week with a word that is derived from the word "Sabbath." (Doug Batchelor, 2011).

Batchelor (2011) provides a possible explanation for this, using Genesis 11 to support his view, with which we concur. This account of the history of man is the first indication of mankind speaking in different languages, after which man populated various parts of the earth. Although their languages were different, one concept remained the same: the Sabbath.

This further supports our premise that the Sabbath is relevant for all mankind, not just Jews and Christians, even today.

This provides a beautiful thought that people realized the importance of dedicating to God a day out of each week, by resting in Him and giving Him glory, all before He found it necessary to make it a requirement in the Ten Commandments.

6

Sabbath Then, Sabbath Now, Sabbath Forever

𝒯he observance of the Sabbath will also be done in eternity, when the New Heaven and the New Earth come. Isaiah 66:22-23 (KJV) states:

> For as the new heavens and the new earth, which I will make, shall remain before me, saith the LORD, so shall your seed and your name remain. And it shall come to pass, [that] from one new moon to another, and from one Sabbath to another, shall all flesh come to worship before me, saith the LORD.

How long was the Sabbath meant to kept? Forever. This is also indicated in Exodus 31:12-18 (KJV):

And the LORD spake unto Moses, saying, Speak thou also unto the children of Israel, saying, Verily my Sabbaths ye shall keep: for it [is] a sign between me and you throughout your generations; that [ye] may know that I [am] the LORD that doth sanctify you. Ye shall keep the Sabbath therefore; for it [is] holy unto you: every one that defileth it shall surely be put to death: for whosoever doeth [any] work therein, that soul shall be cut off from among his people. Six days may work be done; but in the seventh [is] the Sabbath of rest, holy to the LORD: whosoever doeth [any] work in the Sabbath day, he shall surely be put to death. Wherefore the children of Israel shall keep the Sabbath, to observe the Sabbath throughout their generations, [for] a perpetual covenant. It [is] a sign between me and the children of Israel for ever: for [in] six days the LORD made heaven and earth, and on the seventh day he rested, and was refreshed. And he gave unto Moses, when he had made an end of communing with him upon mount Sinai, two tables of testimony, tables of stone, written with the finger of God.

So, as you can see, God gave the Sabbath to be kept then, now, and forever:

Then: God was the first to keep the Sabbath during the first week of creation (Genesis 2:1-3). Later, He gave the command to Moses that it was to be kept by God's chosen people.

- ***Now***: we can see the Sabbath being kept today by Jews and many Christians.
- ***Forever***: God meant the Sabbath to be kept forever as a "perpetual, never-ending covenant."

7

Not the sabbath(s), but THE Sabbath

The word *Sabbath*, as stated in the Fourth Commandment, is the only one in the Bible that is referenced as "THE Sabbath." There are, however, other uses of the word *Sabbath* that do not refer to the Lord's seventh day. What is the difference? Well, first of all, only in the Fourth Commandment does Exodus 31:12-18 state that we are to observe "The Sabbath" forever. All other "sabbaths" were instituted as holy feasts and convocations for the children of Israel and not as a designated day of the week. A holy convocation, for example, can take place on a Thursday or a Friday; however, the Sabbath the Lord requires us to keep by resting can only be observed on the seventh day of the week. In the next chapter, we will explain what we mean by "rest."

8

The Sabbath is a Day for Rest, Not Wrest

e are not only to rest from work on the Sabbath, but more importantly we are to physically, mentally, and emotionally cease all our labors, personal interests, and activities that are not Christ-centered. The question is, "Are you *resting* on the Sabbath, or are you *wresting* on the Sabbath?" The word *rest* means "to relax, take a break, become inactive, to cease from labor." The word *wrest* means "to twist or turn; pull, jerk, or force by a violent twist, to take away by force, to get or take by effort, to turn from the proper course or position."

Some actually wrest on the Sabbath, even though they may not be working in a physical manner. This means they seem to find observing the Sabbath by "Remembering it and to keep it holy" as something arduous to do. *Wrest* is the root word for *wrestling*. Some find themselves in a wrestling match with the idea of keeping the Sabbath, meaning they have to force themselves to keep the day holy by not doing their own pleasures. To accomplish this, they have to pull or jerk themselves into position to honor the Sabbath. Such people find observing the Sabbath to be a violent twist of their own will because it fights (wrestles) against God's will.

Resting from everything includes our worries, thinking about things that cause us stress, and even doing anything that is not related to Christ, even if it's something pleasurable. After all, you deserve a break today and you can experience it by stepping on the brakes, by taking time out to cease from all other labor, both external and internal. This is what the Lord expects us to do when we honor the Fourth Commandment. We must not view observing the Sabbath as an act of compulsion. On the contrary, we must see it as an act of love, a love for God.

Some may not find it difficult to "Remember the Sabbath," but they do find it a laborious task when trying to "keep it holy." This brings us to the final definition for the word *wrest*, which is "to twist or turn from the proper course or position." The main objective of wresting is to twist your opponent into a position they do not want to be in. It's hard work for those who engage in it because it requires using force to get someone to turn from their proper position. Sadly, some find observing the Sabbath as something that causes them to not be in a proper position because it requires forsaking doing their own will to solely honor the Lord for a period of twenty-four hours.

9

Jesus Kept the Sabbath; Jesus is Lord of the Sabbath

*W*hen you study the Sabbath intently, you will see Jesus in all of it because Jesus Christ is the only One who gives us rest. In Matthew 11:28 (KJV), He commands us to go to Him to find it: "Come unto me, all ye that labor and are heavy laden, and I will give you rest." The BBE translation puts it this way: "Come unto me, all you who are troubled and weighted down with care, and I will give you rest." Isn't it wonderful to know we can always find the rest we need in Jesus? God gave the Sabbath to man to rest in Him, and Jesus gives rest to man when we come to Him.

The prescription for obtaining rest in Jesus is found in Matthew 11:29 (KJV): "Take my yoke upon you and learn of me, for I am gentle and humble in heart, and you will find rest for your souls." The Amplified Version says it this way: "Take my yoke upon you and learn from Me [Following Me as My disciple], for I am gentle and humble in heart, and you will find rest (renewal, blessed quiet) for your souls."

Jesus kept the Sabbath throughout His ministry, and you will see this throughout the gospels. This should serve to refute the claim the Sabbath was nullified by Jesus' death on the cross. We also see in the book of Acts, the disciples and the early church continued to keep the Sabbath. If it had been cancelled by Christ's death, they would not have continued to keep it. The Sabbath remains in effect today, tomorrow, and forevermore. So, for us to be like Jesus, we must do what He did and keep the Sabbath.

In addition, Jesus said repeatedly that He is Lord of the Sabbath, and He honored the day by keeping the Sabbath. You would think Jesus would have been exempt from observing the Sabbath because, after all, He was the one who created it. But instead we find He constantly kept it. Now if Jesus, who is Lord even of the Sabbath, which means He is much greater than the day itself, observed it, what do you think He wants us to do? He wants us to keep it just like He did and remember, "He is Lord EVEN of the Sabbath." This is why in the next chapter, we will expound on why observing the Sabbath is one of the greatest sacrifices we can give to the Lord.

10

Observing the Sabbath, One of the Greatest Sacrifices

*A*lthough fasting is something we do as Christians, as it depicts self-denial, even fasting seems like a small sacrifice in comparison to the self-sacrificial denying that takes place as we observe the Sabbath the way God has prescribed us to. When we truly honor the Sabbath by "Remembering it, and by keeping it holy," we are living out Matthew 16:24 (KJV), in which Jesus says to His disciples, "If any [man] will come after me, let him deny himself, and take up his cross, and follow me." We are persuaded that this Scripture depicts observing the Sabbath as one of the greatest sacrifices and acts of holiness we can render to God.

11

From Sacrifice to Sublimity

Anyone who finds the principles of the Sabbath unfamiliar will find it difficult to keep the Sabbath holy. We generally work five days out of our seven-day week. Most people have Saturdays and Sundays off. Sunday Christians go to church on Sunday and Saturday Christians go to church on Saturday. Because we work only five days, we have only one day to do the things we may not have attended to, such as laundry, shopping, cleaning, etc. The sacrifice lies in having one day to attend to these responsibilities instead of two. That being said, we now have a better understanding of why some find it a sacrifice to observe the Sabbath.

A sacrifice is something difficult to give up, something you do not have any extra to spare. This can be time, money, tasks, or whatever you may deem difficult to give up. After the children of Israel left Egypt as slaves, we see the difficulty they had in giving up their time to the Lord. Exodus 16:22-30 (NIV) states:

On the sixth day, they gathered twice as much—two omers for each person—and the leaders of the community came and reported this to Moses. He said to them, "This is what the LORD commanded: 'Tomorrow is to be a day of sabbath rest, a holy sabbath to the LORD. So bake what you want to bake and boil what you want to boil. Save whatever is left and keep it until morning.'" So they saved it until morning, as Moses commanded, and it did not stink or get maggots in it. "Eat it today," Moses said, "because today is a sabbath to the LORD. You will not find any of it on the ground today. Six days you are to gather it, but on the seventh day, the Sabbath, there will not be any."

Nevertheless, some of the people went out on the seventh day to gather it, but they found none. Then the LORD said to Moses, "How long will you refuse to keep my commands and my instructions? Bear in mind that the LORD has given you the Sabbath; that is why on the sixth day he gives you bread for two days. Everyone is to stay where they are on the seventh day; no one is to go out." So the people rested on the seventh day.

The children of Israel were slaves in Egypt for more than 400 years, before God had given them the Moral and Mosaic Law. Prior to this, the concept of Sabbath rest was not understood as a time of freedom from work and devotion to God. While they were enslaved in Egypt, the children of Israel worked under strenuous conditions while under the yoke of bondage.

The Sabbath was actually a gift from God to them because for one day each week they were not required to work as they had been while they were under a cruel task master. Unfortunately, because of their enslavement they found it difficult not to work. So obeying God's commandment to rest necessitated an element of trust, and they simply did not trust God. As we know from enslaved cultures throughout history, it is difficult to recondition the mind of a slave. So, these former slaves gathered their food as they did any other day.

God gives us this same gift of rest today, which for New Testament believers is two-fold. The Sabbath is a day of rest and repose from our physical work in addition to the ultimate spiritual rest we have in Jesus. Because of His finished work on the cross, we do not need to labor for our salvation, our peace, or everlasting life. Jesus did all the work for us and we can therefore rest assured that we are protected and well cared for. We can and should just rest in the Lord.

Unfortunately many today are still like the children of Israel because they feel it is a sacrifice to stop doing the things they want and need to do. In this respect, keeping the Sabbath can be difficult because the minds of such people are on all the things they must do in their lives and not on Jesus.

We have found, however, that keeping the Sabbath is not a sacrifice, but a celebration as Isaiah 58:13 says it should be. It is a day to celebrate the awesomeness and wonder of God. Consider the fact that Jesus gives us the strength, intellect, and creativity to work for six days, and on the seventh day, we can rest and have the opportunity to do as God did after His finished creation: He admired His own work and said it was good.

We should, therefore, do as God did and reflect on the blessings of being able to work, and praise Him for that ability. We should be grateful to the Lord for being successful in our work, as it is He who gives us the power to achieve great things and excel in our labors. In doing this, we are celebrating what the Lord has done through and for us. We are acknowledging the omnipotence of God and rejoicing in His glory.

Once you truly immerse yourself in observing the Sabbath the Lord's way, and experience all the spiritual and physical blessings that come as a result of it, you will move from seeing the Sabbath as a sacrifice to seeing it as sublime. The word *sublime* means "something that transcends greatness or beauty for the observer." When something is truly wonderful, or someone acts in a noble way, it's sublime. The Latin root, *sublimis*, means "uplifted, high, or exalted." When you observe the Sabbath with your whole heart, mind, and soul, you will discover the greatness and the beauty of it. This experience will uplift you and take you to a higher place in your relationship with Christ, just like it did for us.

12

For God So Loved the World, He Gave Us the Sabbath

*J*esus is our Sabbath rest. One of the names for Jesus is "the Prince of Peace," as found in Isaiah 9:6. This means Jesus is our peace. He gives us what He is, which is peace. When we have peace, we are definitely in a state of rest from worries, troubles, problems, and strife. While you will experience these things in life, you will have a peace that gives you the ability to rest in the fact that God is with you, as stated in Philippians 4:7 (NKJV): "and the peace of God, which surpasses all understanding, will guard your hearts and minds through Christ Jesus."

13

Who Else Kept the Sabbath?

*B*ecause the Lord has expected all of us throughout time to "Remember the Sabbath by keeping it holy," some key biblical figures in addition to God Himself have also kept the Sabbath. These include the disciples, before and after Christ died; the first-century church; many others who were prominent throughout the Old and New Testaments.

The Sabbath will also be kept when God creates the new Heaven and the new Earth, as we noted earlier in Isaiah 66:22-23. Because we are the spiritual descendants of Israel, and therefore related to Abraham by faith (as stated in Romans 4:9-12), we are mandated by God to keep the Sabbath forever. The New Living Translation makes this principle even clearer:

> Now, is this blessing only for the Jews, or is it also for uncircumcised Gentiles? Well, we have been saying that Abraham was counted

as righteous by God because of his faith. But how did this happen? Was he counted as righteous only after he was circumcised, or was it before he was circumcised? Clearly, God accepted Abraham before he was circumcised! Circumcision was a sign that Abraham already had faith and that God had already accepted him and declared him to be righteous—even before he was circumcised. So, Abraham is the spiritual father of those who have faith but have not been circumcised. They are counted as righteous because of their faith. And Abraham is also the spiritual father of those who have been circumcised, but only if they have the same kind of faith Abraham had before he was circumcised.

Since the Lord says we are the "spiritual children of Israel," therefore, we are admonished to obey the command to keep the Sabbath. Exodus 31:16 (KJV) says, "Wherefore the children of Israel shall keep the Sabbath, to observe the Sabbath throughout their generations, [for] a perpetual covenant." The New Living Translation says it this way: "The people of Israel must keep the Sabbath day by observing it from generation to generation. This is a covenant obligation for all time."

14

There Was More Than One Law

It is imperative to understand and recognize there are noticeable differences between the Ten Commandments, which were written by "the finger of God," also known as the Moral Law, and the Ceremonial Law, also known as the Law of Moses or the Mosaic Covenant. We have found many scriptures to support our premise that the Moral and Mosaic Laws were distinctly separate. We have also found biblical evidence proving the Mosaic Covenant, along with all its ordinances and statutes, ended when Jesus died on the cross. Jesus' death did fulfill (cancel) the Mosaic Law, but not the Moral Law, which is the Ten Commandments. We will show you in the Bible that the Ten Commandments have not and will not end, and they are still in effect for every one of us to keep today.

In Deuteronomy 4:13-14, Moses explained to the people that his Law was different from God's Moral Law. Deuteronomy 4:13 (KJV) says:

And he declared unto you his covenant, which
he commanded you to perform, even ten commandments; and he wrote them upon two tables
of stone. And the Lord commanded me at that
time to teach you statutes and judgments, that
ye might do them in the land whither ye go over
to possess it.

After Moses clearly says in this text, "He [God] declared
to you his covenant, which he commanded you to perform,
even ten commandments," he says the Lord commanded
him to teach the people his covenant, referring to the Mosaic
Covenant, which comprised the statues and judgments of the
Law of Moses. This covenant consisted of the "handwriting
of ordinances that were against us," which Jesus "blotted
out" (canceled and freed us from) when He died on the cross,
according to Colossians 2:14. Note how three different trans-
lations express this truth:

"Blotting out the handwriting of ordinances
that was against us, which was contrary to
us, and took it out of the way, nailing it to his
cross;" (KJV)

"Having canceled the charge of our legal
indebtedness, which stood against us and condemned us; he has taken it away, nailing it to
the cross." (NIV)

"Having put an end to the handwriting of the law, which was against us, taking it out of the way by nailing it to his cross;" (BBE)

Crews (2007), author of *Feast Days & Sabbaths: Are They Still Binding?* gives some interesting insights regarding the vast differences between the Ten Commandments (Moral Law) and the Mosaic Covenant (Ceremonial Law):

> God answers that important question in such a way that no doubt can remain. "Neither will I make the feet of Israel move any more out of the land which I gave their fathers; only if they will observe to do according to all that I have commanded them and according to all the law that my servant Moses commanded them" (2 Kings 21:8). Here we are assured that the statutes which Moses gave the people were called a "law." God speaks of the law "I commanded" and also the "law ... Moses commanded." Unless this truth is understood properly, limitless confusion will result. Daniel was inspired to make the same careful distinction when he prayed for the desolated sanctuary of his scattered nation. "Yea, all Israel have transgressed thy law, even by departing, that they might not obey thy voice; therefore, the curse is poured upon us, and the oath that is written in the law of Moses the

servant of God, because we have sinned against him" (Daniel 9:11). Once more we see "thy law" and "the law of Moses," and this time the two are recognized as different in content. There are no curses recorded in the Ten Commandments that God wrote, but the law which Moses wrote contained an abundance of such curses and judgments. No one can confuse this writing with the way the Mosaic Law was produced. "And Moses wrote this law ... And it came to pass, when Moses had made an end of writing the words of this law in a book, until they were finished, That Moses commanded the Levites, which bare the ark of the covenant of the Lord, saying, Take this book of the law, and put it in the side of the ark of the covenant of the Lord your God, that it may be there for a witness against thee" (Deuteronomy 31:9, 24-26). This book of statutes and judgments which Moses wrote in a book was placed in a pocket on the side of the ark. In contrast, the law written by God on tables of stone was placed inside the ark of the covenant. "And thou shalt put into the ark the testimony which I shall give thee" (Exodus 25:16).

Crews goes on to give the reason God even allowed the Mosaic Covenant (Ceremonial Law), which was clearly "against us," to come into existence, and that reason was sin:

"Because they ... had polluted my Sabbaths, and their eyes were after their fathers' idols. Wherefore I gave them also statutes that were not good, and judgments whereby they should not live" (Ezekiel 20:24-25). Observe carefully how the prophet identifies the Sabbath law, and then immediately says, "I gave them ALSO statutes that were not good." Keep in mind that the Ten Commandments were called "holy, and just, and good" (Romans 7:12). Because of its curses and judgments against their continual disobedience, the law of Moses was "against" them and was "not good."

After reading these texts, we have come to recognize there are clear distinctions between the Moral and Mosaic Laws. We believe if you pray and intensively study these Scriptures, you will definitely be able to see these stark differences as well.

15

Do You Practice "Ceremonial-ism?"

eremonialism … What is that? We know there is no such word, but it is a word the Holy Spirit gave us to demonstrate a specific idea as we constantly witnessed many engaging in this practice. *Ceremonialism* describes Christians of today who keep the Ceremonial Law along with the Moral Law (the Ten Commandments). This was the way the children of Israel practiced the Law before the death of Jesus. Now, this type of lifestyle is not merited, nor is it necessary. When Jesus died, He had completely met all the requirements to fulfill the entire Ceremonial (Mosaic) Law, something no man could ever do. Since this is true, why then is there a need to still keep the Ceremonial Law? Jesus clearly eradicated the need for us to do it any longer.

People who practice "ceremonialism" commonly say things like, "We must still keep the Sabbath, even today, because Jesus' death on the cross did not do away with the Ten Commandments," which is emphatically true. Those same individuals, however, practice some of the ceremonial rituals that Jesus' death on the cross did eradicate and set us free from. Under the Mosaic Covenant, for example, circumcision was a requirement for the life of any male child of Israel. Genesis 17:13-14 (NKJV) says:

> He who is born in your house and he who is bought with your money must be circumcised, and My covenant shall be in your flesh for an everlasting covenant. And the uncircumcised male child, who is not circumcised in the flesh of his foreskin, that person shall be cut off from his people; he has broken My covenant.

Jesus' work on the cross did away with this form of circumcision. Galatians 5:6 (KJV) states, "For in Jesus Christ neither circumcision availeth anything, nor uncircumcision; but faith which worketh by love." Please know that we are not condemning circumcision in itself. It is a custom practiced in many cultures. It is also believed to have health benefits. But it is no longer a requirement for us to be in a relationship with God.

Furthermore, Jesus' death on the cross freed us from the bondage of keeping the Ceremonial Law. Deuteronomy 31:9, 24-26 (NIV) states:

> And Moses wrote this law ... And it came to pass, when Moses had made an end of writing the words of this law in a book, until they were finished, That Moses commanded the Levites, which bare the ark of the covenant of the Lord, saying, Take this book of the law, and put it in the side of the ark of the covenant of the Lord your God, that it may be there for a witness against thee.

This book of statutes and judgments that Moses wrote in a book was placed in a pocket on the side of the ark. In contrast, the law written by God, on tables of stone, was placed inside the ark of the covenant. Exodus 25:16 (KJV) says, "And thou shalt put into the ark the testimony which I shall give thee."

When we practice ceremonialism, we are in essence negating the important work the Lord did on the cross. Romans 7:4 (NLT) states, "So, my dear brothers and sisters, this is the point: You died to the power of the law when you died with Christ." Note other New Testament Scriptures that add to what Romans 7:4 says:

> John 1:17 (KJV): "For the law [not the Moral Law of the Ten Commandments] was given by Moses, [but] grace and truth came by Jesus Christ."

> Romans 8:3-4 (KJV): "For what the law could not do, in that it was weak through the flesh,

God sending his own Son in the likeness of sinful flesh, and for sin, condemned sin in the flesh: That the righteousness of the law might be fulfilled in us, who walk not after the flesh, but after the Spirit."

Romans 8:3-4 (NLT): "The law of Moses was unable to save us because of the weakness of our sinful nature. So, God did what the law could not do. He sent his own Son in a body like the body's we sinners have. And in that body God declared an end to sin's control over us by giving his Son as a sacrifice for our sins. He did this so that the just requirement of the law would be fully satisfied for us, who no longer follow our sinful nature but instead follow the Spirit."

16

Worship God, Not the Sabbath

*W*hile God gave us the Sabbath as a day to rest and worship, it was certainly not given as a day *to be worshipped*. God alone, who is the Lord Jesus Christ, is the only one worthy of our worship. For even when John attempted to worship the angel he encountered in Revelation 22:8-9 (NIV), Jesus clearly instructed him to reserve his worship only for God:

> I, John, am the one who heard and saw these things. And when I had heard and seen them, I fell down to worship at the feet of the angel who had been showing them to me. But he said to me, "Don't do that! I am a fellow servant with you and with your fellow prophets and with all who keep the words of this scroll. Worship God!"

As Christians, we must not worship the Sabbath, but we should worship Jesus *on* the Sabbath. Luke 4:8 (KJV) says, "And Jesus answered Thou shalt worship the Lord thy God, and him only shalt thou serve."

Some mistakenly make the Sabbath, not Jesus, the center and most important aspect of their lives. While a person can "Remember the Sabbath to keep it holy," if they are not "born again of the water and of the Spirit," (saved) as stated in John 3:3 and 3:5, keeping the Sabbath will not get them to Heaven because it has no power to save.

During Jesus' night encounter with Nicodemus in John 3:3 and 3:5 (KJV), he said to him, "...Verily, verily, I say unto thee, except a man be born again, he cannot see the kingdom of God." He adds in John 3:5, "...Verily, verily, I say unto thee, except a man be born of water and [of] the Spirit, he cannot enter into the kingdom of God."

So, only Jesus can save us. If we place the same emphasis on pleasing, reverencing, and honoring Jesus in the same manner that we do the Sabbath day, our walks with Christ, the one who made the Sabbath, will be much closer, stronger, and intimate, just the way He wants it to be.

Section 2

A Historical Overview of
the Evolution of the Sabbath

In this section, we will discuss why the majority of Christians observe the Sabbath on Sunday instead of Saturday. We will also cover who changed the Sabbath from Saturday to Sunday, why it changed, and the effect of that change on Christians today.

17

The Consequences of Constantine

The answer to the question, "Why are we calling Sunday the Sabbath?" begins in the early days of the church's history. For many years, Jewish and Gentile Christians were persecuted by the Romans. Eventually, the Gentile Christians felt the necessity to distance themselves from their Jewish Christian brethren.

At the beginning of the fourth century, Emperor Constantine professed to have converted to Christianity. He was originally a sun worshiper, who worshiped on Sunday, the first day of the week. This influence of regular Sunday worship undoubtably prompted his decision to change the Christian Sabbath from Saturday to Sunday. He passed a law in 321 AD, proclaiming that Sunday would be a day of rest and no work was to be done.

Because certain Gentile Christians were already seeking dissociation with Jewish Christians, they embraced this new day of worship. As a result, they were no longer persecuted as their Jewish fellow Christians (Gibbon 1960). Many Gentile Christians, however, continued to keep the seventh day (Saturday) as the Sabbath until about 364 AD when, according to the Catechism of the Catholic Church, Section 2, Article 3 (1994), the Council of Laodicea took responsibility for changing the Christian Sabbath from Saturday to Sunday, stating the Church has the authority to supersede the Bible. Thus, all Christians began to worship on Sunday, calling it the "Lord's Day" and the Christian Sabbath.

18

Tradition Verses Truth

In light of this significant piece of church history, we now pose a question: "Just because we have been calling Sunday the Sabbath for over 1500 years, does this make it right?" We would like to answer this question by making two points. First, we often do things out of our commitment to tradition, not fully understanding why they are done. Many traditions, such as this one, have their roots in dark circumstances.

Second, the Catholic Council superseding biblical authority is completely unscriptural. Revelation 22:18-19 (ESV) says:

> I warn everyone who hears the words of the prophecy of this book: if anyone adds to them, God will add to him the plagues described in this book, and if anyone takes away from the words of the book of this prophecy, God will

take away his share in the tree of life and in the
holy city, which are described in this book.

In changing the Sabbath to Sunday, the council added their
own will and desire to God's already-established command.

19

Man Changed the Times, Not God

*M*any practices followed by some Christians today are manmade and not God inspired, yet these Christians are still keeping them because they've always followed the traditions and rituals, which are not based on scripture. Daniel 7:25 (NIV) warns us that one of the antichrist's goals during his reign will be to change times: "He will speak against the Most High and oppress his holy people and try to change the set times and the laws." For the most part, the entire world, including many Christians, have adapted to following Constantine's blatant act of changing the Sabbath to Sunday.

Troy Miller (2019) says in an article entitled, "Constantine Changed Calendar," which he wrote for Light Bearer Ministries.org:

> In 321 AD, the Emperor Constantine the Great permanently grafted the astrological plane-tary week system onto the Roman calendar,

making the first day of this new week the day of the Sun and a day of rest and worship for all, and imposing the sequence and names to the days of the planetary week as we know them today. With this official edict the market week and the planetary week were finally and permanently fused into one continuous seven-day cycle named after the "gods." By edict of the Emperor, Roman-Babylonish time was suddenly transformed into "Christian" time. While there were holdouts for a while, the new Roman system of time was adopted throughout most of western Europe: in the Germanic languages, such as Old English.

Following is a chart of the Roman gods for which each day of the week is named:

Planetary "god"	Latin Germanic "god"	Modern English	Modern Italian
Sun	Solis	Sunday	domenica
Moon	Lunae	Monday	lunedi
Mars	Martis	Tuesday	martedì
Mercury	Mercurii	Wednesday	mercoledì
Jupiter	Jovis	Thursday	giovedì
Venus	Veneris	Friday	venerdì
Saturn	Saturni	Saturday	sabato

All this should be sufficient to demonstrate that the week we are so familiar with today, originated as an amalgamation of paganism and commercialism. In fact, the pagan origin of the planetary week is still to be seen in the names of the days of the week in use today.

Thomsen (2003) wrote in her article, "What Day is the Sabbath and Does it Really Matter?" to affirm how even the Catholic Church admits it changed the Sabbath from Saturday to Sunday by its own authority:

> The Catechism recalls the ceremony with which God made known His Law, containing the blessing of the seventh-day Sabbath, by which all humanity is to be judged. Contrast this with the unannounced, unnoticed anticlimax with which the church gradually adopted Sunday at the command of "Christian" emperors and Roman bishops. And these freely admit they made the change from Sabbath (Saturday) to Sunday.

In the *Convert's Catechism of Catholic Doctrine*, we read:

Q. Which is the Sabbath day?

A. Saturday is the Sabbath day.

Q. Why do we observe Sunday instead of Saturday?

A. We observe Sunday instead of Saturday because the Catholic Church, in the Council of Laodicea, (336 AD) transferred the solemnity from Saturday to Sunday....

Q. Why did the Catholic Church substitute Sunday for Saturday?

A. The Church substituted Sunday for Saturday because Christ rose from the dead on a Sunday, and the Holy Ghost descended upon the Apostles on a Sunday.

Q. By what authority did the Church substitute Sunday for Saturday?

A. The Church substituted Sunday for Saturday by the plenitude of that divine power which Jesus Christ bestowed upon her!

—Rev. Peter Geiermann, C.SS.R., (1946), p. 50.

In *An Abridgment of the Christian Doctrine*:

Q. How prove you that the Church hath power to command feasts and holy days?

A. By the very act of changing the Sabbath into Sunday, which Protestants allow, and therefore they fondly contradict themselves by keeping Sunday strictly and breaking most other feasts commanded by the same Church.

Q. How prove you that?

A. Because by keeping Sunday, they acknowledge the Church's power to ordain feasts and to command them under sin, and by not keeping the rest [of the feasts] by her command, they again deny, in fact, the same power.

–Rev. Henry Tuberville, D.D. (R.C.), (1833), page 58.

In *A Doctrinal Catechism:*

Q. Have you any other way of proving the Church has power to institute festivals of precept?

A. Had she not such power, she could not have done that in which all modern religionists agree with her. She could not have substituted the observance of Sunday, the first day of the week, for the observance of Saturday, the seventh day, a change for which there is no scriptural authority.

Ultimately the Bible is clear that the seventh day is the Sabbath:

"And God blessed the seventh day and made it holy" (Genesis 2:3).

"Therefore the Lord blessed the Sabbath day and made it holy" (Exodus 20:11).

If God intended another day to become the Sabbath, He must have removed the blessing from the seventh day and placed it on the day that was to replace it. But when God bestows a blessing, it is forever:

"...You, O Lord, have blessed it, and it will be blessed forever" (1 Chronicles 17:27).

"I have received a command to bless; He has blessed, and I cannot change it" (Numbers 23:20).

Your birthday, a memorial of your birth, cannot be changed, though you may celebrate it on a different day. Neither can the Sabbath, a memorial of creation (Exodus 20:11), be changed, though some may celebrate it on a different day.

Now that we know this information, it is our responsibility to examine the error of the traditional way of Sabbath observance and compare it to the truth of God's Word regarding His holy day: truth that has been established since the first week of the creation of the world.

20

Why the Devil Doesn't Want Us To Keep the Sabbath

*N*ow that we see how we have come to worship on Sunday, let us examine some other possible hidden reasons this holy day was changed. When we think of the Sabbath, we think of two verbs: "to remember" and "to keep."

To Remember

In remembering the Sabbath, we turn our attention to God and what was done on that day. He rested. He created rest on the seventh day; therefore, the principle of rest is part of creation. In remembering this fact, we see the necessity of calming our minds and hearts and refraining from all elements of work. Satan does not want us to rest our bodies and our spirits, because we will able to hear from the Lord more freely.

Without the concerns of our weekly responsibilities, we are at liberty to receive the restoration, rejuvenation, and repose that comes from Jesus. With renewed spirits, we are able to accomplish God's will for our lives in a way that is more glorifying to Him. But we can only come to this state if we are in a position of resting. This is why Satan does not want us to "remember" this holy day.

To Keep

In keeping the day holy, we are not doing our own business. Instead we are doing the business of Christ. This comes in the form of showing love, serving others, and worshipping God, all of which displease Satan.

By resting and doing the work of the Lord, we see the glorious ways God can be magnified on Saturdays. If all creations would honor the Sabbath as stated in the Word, the Lord would be lifted high in the earth. This is why the devil has fought so hard to make us forget this day. In doing so, he has encouraged us to work on the Sabbath, disregarding our physical and spiritual need for rest.

21

The Difference Between the Sabbath and Every Other Weekday

*T*his is one of the greatest debated questions when discussing the Sabbath. Should it be observed only on that one day of the week, or every day? The answer to this question can be proven both biblically and historically.

We have heard many Christians say, "I don't need a special day to observe the Sabbath. I keep every day holy." We do not doubt that these sincere Christians do keep every day holy. We should consider every day holy because we are holy people with holy mindsets. We should be lifting up the name of Jesus and keeping Him first in our lives every day. Nevertheless, there must be a distinguishing factor that makes the Sabbath different from all other days. What is that factor? The Lord states it clearly, "work." The work factor is why God established the Sabbath.

The Work Factor

Resting from our weekly labors and devoting the entire day to repose, reflection, and remembering the Lord, is something we do not do every day. We cannot be in a total state of rest day because we have to attend to the various duties that keep us alive. We have to work. The Bible makes this declaration, "if we do not work, we should not eat" (2 Thessalonians 3:10, NIV).

We know from a practical standpoint that it is impossible to be preoccupied with work and our other personal cares and activities while exclusively reverencing the Lord. We cannot give Him our total undivided attention as we should do and as we are commanded to do on the Sabbath. No one can do this each and every day, so it is only right to give the Lord the one day a week He requires. He still mandates us to keep the Sabbath, to pause and cease from all other labors and devote our full time and attention to Him.

In keeping the Sabbath, we stop working. In its place, we are lifting up Jesus and keeping our minds stayed on Him, without the concerns of the many obligations we have during the week. This is what makes the Sabbath different, holy, and set apart from all other days. Consequently, we say to those Christians who keep the Sabbath every day, "Are you truly keeping the Sabbath?" And we all know the answer to that question, an emphatic NO!

22

The Strongest Proof in the New Testament For Keeping the Sabbath Today

*T*here are many who believe the New Testament never says God commands us to keep the Sabbath today. But there are many references in the New Testament that affirm the Sabbath must still be observed, and the greatest proof of this can be found in Hebrews 4:1-11 (NIV):

> Therefore, since the promise of entering his rest still stands, let us be careful that none of you be found to have fallen short of it. ² For we also have had the good news proclaimed to us, just as they did; but the message they heard was of no value to them, because they did not share the

faith of those who obeyed. ³ Now we who have
believed enter that rest, just as God has said,

"So I declared on oath in my anger,
  'They shall never enter my rest.'"

And yet his works have been finished since the
creation of the world. ⁴ For somewhere he has
spoken about the seventh day in these words:
"On the seventh day God rested from all his
works." ⁵ And again in the passage above he
says, "They shall never enter my rest."

⁶ Therefore since it still remains for some to
enter that rest, and since those who formerly
had the good news proclaimed to them did not
go in because of their disobedience, ⁷ God again
set a certain day, calling it "Today." This he did
when a long time later he spoke through David,
as in the passage already quoted:

"Today, if you hear his voice,
  do not harden your hearts."

⁸ For if Joshua had given them rest, God would
not have spoken later about another day. ⁹ There
remains, then, a Sabbath-rest for the people of
God; ¹⁰ for anyone who enters God's rest also

rests from their works, just as God did from his.
¹¹ Let us, therefore, make every effort to enter
that rest, so that no one will perish by following
their example of disobedience.

Let us examine a few of these verses in greater detail.

Verse 1

"Therefore, since the promise of entering his rest
still stands, let us be careful that none of you be
found to have fallen short of it."

It still stands, and that is that. We, the children of God,
must continue to embrace and adhere to keeping the Sabbath.
The Sabbath is God's eternal promise. It is His unending and
never-changing contract agreement for His children to keep
forever. Exodus 31:16 (KJV) says, "Wherefore the children of
Israel shall keep the Sabbath, to observe the Sabbath throughout
their generations, [for] a perpetual covenant." This shows us
the Lord did not change His mind regarding His promise and
His command for us to keep the Sabbath.

We must clearly heed to the latter clause of verse 1: "let us
be careful that none of you be found to have fallen short of it."
Here the writer stresses to us to be "careful." The word *careful*
is defined as being "cautious in one's actions, to be exact,
thorough, solicitously mindful, precise, deliberate, vigilant,

particular, and observant." He wants us not to miss the mark by "falling short of it."

What the Lord does not want us to "fall short of" is "not to enter into His rest." Of course He is talking about His Sabbath rest. The Lord still wants us to "Remember the Sabbath to keep it holy." It is time for every one of us to take heed to His word because we do not want to be guilty of "falling short of it." Let us be obedient to fulfill and carry out what God commands us to carry out because as we "enter into the Sabbath rest" we shall most certainly be blessed.

Verse 2

> "For we also have had the good news proclaimed to us, just as they did; but the message they heard was of no value to them, because they did not share the faith of those who obeyed." The KJV says it this way: "For unto us was the gospel preached, as well as unto them: but the word preached did not profit them, not being mixed with faith in them that heard it."

The writer is pointing out they all had the same gospel message spoken to them. They all heard the exact same word of the Lord, but because they did not allow what they heard to be received and taken in with faith, they did not obey it. Obey what, you ask? They did not obey and adhere to His command to "enter the Sabbath rest." It takes more than just having a mindset of not working on the Sabbath to honor it; it truly takes having faith in God to obey the commandment to "Remember the Sabbath, to keep it holy."

When it comes to having true faith in God, we know it is much more than just saying mere words; it is only when we put our faith into action that God accepts it. As we all know, the Lord does not *hear* faith; He wants to *see* it practiced by those of us who say we are His children. Yes, God wants to see your faith in Him.

Two scriptural reference solidify this point. Just before Jesus healed the paralyzed man who was carried by four men in Mark 2:5 (NIV), it says, "When Jesus saw their faith...." So, we can see the Lord is not interested in just hearing our words of faith to Him; He wants to SEE our faith in Him.

It was when Jesus saw the faith of those who had brought the paralyzed man put into action that He proceeded to heal the man. We must do the same thing these four men did. We must allow God to see that we truly have faith in Him. James 2:20, 26 (KJV) says to us, "that faith without works is dead." This simply means the Lord want us to "Put up or shut up" as the old saying goes. When it comes to observing the Sabbath, God is not interested in the words that come from our lips; He definitely looks at the actions that come from our hearts.

Jesus affirms this when He says, "These people honor me with their lips, but their hearts are far from me" (Matthew 15:8, NIV). It is imperative that we observe the Sabbath by doing it, not just by saying it. Heeding the Fourth Commandment properly is all about doing, not just talking about it. If people spend as much time keeping the Sabbath as they do debating the issue and trying to rationalize why they should not keep the Sabbath, they would have a more solid relationship with Jesus. As Hebrews 4:2 says, the "gospel message" they all heard was of "no value" or "profit to them, because they did not receive the word with faith." In other words, to hear the word and not have faith in it is not beneficial. Let us all take heed to the words that James 1:22 (KJV) instructs us to carry out, which is to "be ye doers of the word, and not hearers only, deceiving your own selves."

This proves it takes more than just a mere love for God to keep the Sabbath. It also takes faith. The reason so many people do not observe the Sabbath according to God's prescribed standards is because they do not have the faith to do it. As Christians, we know the most essential element for us to have is our faith. Did you know that anyone operating without faith makes the only thing that is impossible for God to do actually happen? And that is for God to be pleased with us. Remember what Hebrews 11:6 says, "But without faith [it is] impossible to please Him (God)." God is not pleased when Christians do not keep the Sabbath, and He is not pleased whenever we do not have or put our faith in Him.

If we truly have faith in God, we will carry out what He has called and commands us to do. We can only show God we have faith in Him (His Word) by acting on it, by doing what He ask us to do. We cannot satisfy the Lord just by hearing His word. James 1:22 (KJV) says, "But be ye doers of the word, and not hearers only, deceiving your own selves." Many are deceived today, especially as it pertains to them not "Remembering the Sabbath and keeping it holy."

Verse 3

> "Now we who have believed enter that rest, just
> as God has said."

This verse lets us know that true believers in Jesus Christ who "have believed enter that rest, just as God has said." Believers will be sure to go into and take the commanded "Sabbath rest."

Verse 4

> God has spoken about the seventh day in these
> words: "On the seventh day God rested from
> all His works."

Notice the text states that God rested from all His works "On the seventh day," (Saturday), not on Sunday, the day the Bible refers to as "the first day of the week." Only Saturday is the day the Bible speaks of whenever they obeyed the Fourth Commandment. Remember, God did not change this day; only man, Constantine, changed the day from Saturday to Sunday.

Even after the resurrection of Jesus, in the book of Acts, verses (13:27, 13:42, 13:44, 15:21, 16:13, 17:2, and 18:4) the disciples kept the seventh day (Saturday). Although it may sound good in theory, the resurrection of Christ did not change the Sabbath day. We should obey God over man any day.

Verse 4 also makes clear what God rested from: "On the seventh day God rested from all his works [plural]."

Verse 6

> "Therefore, since it still remains, for some to enter that rest, and since those who formerly had the good news proclaimed to them did not go in because of their disobedience."

Just as we saw in verse 1, we see the word "still" once again, in "it still remains." What "still remains"? The mandate for us to continue to obey the Fourth Commandment that lovingly requires us to observe the never-ending covenant of keeping the Sabbath. This, as well as the other nine commandments found in God's Moral Law of the Ten Commandments, "still remains" in effect for us to live by today. The Lord requires us to "still enter that rest."

The word *remain* is defined as to "go on, linger, continue, endure, persist, last, reside, tarry, abide, outlast, hold over, and stay over." God is simply saying the Sabbath is something He wants us to keep doing.

The Word of God further states, "and since those who formerly had the good news proclaimed to them did not go in because of their disobedience." They did not enter into the Lord's Sabbath rest because "of their disobedience." When we do not observe the Sabbath, even today, we are acting in disobedience, which is sin (Romans 5:19). Even for those who hear the gospel, the word of God, if we do not take heed to it and apply it to our lives, we are disobeying the Lord, which will in turn cause us to miss the true blessings God has for us.

Verse 7

"God again set a certain day, calling it 'Today.'
This he did when a long time later he spoke
through David in the passage already quoted:
'Today, if you hear his voice, do not harden
your hearts.'"

This text is powerful because it plainly tells us "Today," not tomorrow, but "Today," "if you hear his [God's] voice, do not harden your hearts." When someone operates with a heart that is hardened, the way Pharaoh did, they are acting in disobedience to God to the fullest extent possible. This is living in a manner that is contrary to the way the Lord desires for us to live. Any time we do this, we are sinning against God.

Verse 9

"There remains, then, a Sabbath-rest for the
people of God."

This verse reiterates the "Sabbath rest." The text makes it clear that God requires us to keep "a Sabbath rest" and that this command "still remains" in effect today. It is the "rest" He wants us, His people, to enter into.

Verse 10

"for anyone who enters God's rest also rests
from their works, just as God did from his."

Once again, the Lord is saying in order "to enter God's rest," we must "rest from our works, just as God did from His." This simply means we are required keep the Sabbath. No one is exempt from keeping it.

We should be doing everything God did and those things He commands us to do because we should want to be like God, just as we are admonished to do in Ephesians 5:1 (NKJV): "Therefore be imitators of God as dear children."

With that in mind, this text says, "anyone who enters God's Sabbath rest also rests [ceases, stops] from their own works, just as God rested from His." His what? His works. If we want to be like God then we will rest from our works on the Sabbath just as God did from His.

Verse 11

> "Let us, therefore, make every effort to enter that
> rest, so that no one will perish by following their
> example of disobedience."

As you are reading this book, we urge you to wholeheartedly pay attention to what the Lord, and not just to what we are saying to you, in a personal way. You have to "make every effort to enter that rest," the rest of the Sabbath. God truly wants you and me to observe the Sabbath by resting on it. Note how the Bible says we must "enter that rest." The word *enter* means "to go in, get in, step into, go inside of, make an entrance in, move in, or to penetrate." As we can see, the Lord requires us to "make every effort" to do these things, "to enter that rest."

23

Although Jesus Gives Us Rest, We Still Have to Keep the Sabbath

*T*here are those who quote Matthew 11:28-30 to defend their reason for not observing the Sabbath today. They say it's because "Jesus gives us rest and I find my rest in Him, so why should I have to keep the Sabbath?" This is a good question and we would like to answer it in the manner the Lord gave us.

We absolutely believe Jesus Christ is the ultimate giver of rest, without any doubt at all. We are both witnesses to this fact. Ever since we gave our hearts to Christ, we have experienced such a peace and rest that we had never encountered before we were born again. Although this is true, even today, we still must "enter into that rest, the rest of the Sabbath."

Once again, the proof for this is found in Hebrews 4:1-11. The book of Hebrews was written after the Gospels, which must be taken into consideration to comprehend our point. Jesus stated in Matthew 11:28-30 (NLT):

> Then Jesus said, Come to me, all of you who are weary and carry heavy burdens, and I will give you rest. Take my yoke upon you. Let me teach you, because I am humble and gentle at heart, and you will find rest for your souls. For my yoke is easy to bear, and the burden I give you is light.

Since the gospels were written long before the book of Hebrews, why would the writer of Hebrews say to "make every effort to enter that rest"? We know the text is referring to us entering the Sabbath rest, where we cease from our labors, specifically on the Sabbath day, the seventh day of the week. The question for consideration is, why would the writer of Hebrews command us to do this if only coming to Christ was enough to give us all the rest we need? The writer of Hebrews certainly knew those who came to Christ and received His great salvation also received "rest for their weary souls," yet he was compelled to still admonish us to "make every effort to enter into that rest." This is the same rest he mentioned in verse 10, which says, "for anyone who enters God's rest also rests from their works, just as God did from his."

Hebrews 4:1 says, "Therefore, since the promise of entering his rest still stands, let us be careful that none of you be found to have fallen short of it." Keep in mind this was written after

Jesus made His declarations that He would "give us rest," and that we can "find rest for our weary souls in Him." The writer still found it necessary to inform us that it is our God-given duty and responsibility to make an asserted effort to enter that Sabbath rest. Even those who have received Jesus as Lord of their lives must still not "fall short," or miss out on, entering into the Sabbath rest. Hebrews 4:3-4 proves that even those of us who are saved and have a personal relationship with Christ are still not exempt from entering into the rest of keeping the Sabbath.

24

Keep the Sabbath Because of Love, Not Law

Keeping the Sabbath should not be a task, because that is considered work. There is no doubt the children of Israel loved the Lord, even though they made poor choices, as we still do today. But they were obligated to keep the Sabbath because it is not only part of the Moral Law, but it is also part of the Mosaic Law. Keeping the Sabbath in this manner can become burdensome and ritualistic. A beautiful expression of gratitude and admiration for the Lord can lose its passion when there are too many directives and regulations attached to it. This is what happened in the lives of the children of Israel as it relates to the Sabbath.

This very thing also happened when the Pharisees rebuked Jesus for doing wonderful things for people in need. He performed a few of His miracles on the seventh day and the Jewish leaders resented Him for it. Rather than celebrating in the power and might of Jesus' majesty, they resented and chastised Him for breaking the Sabbath. They were keeping the Sabbath because it was the Law, not out of love. Jesus' acts of healing people on the Sabbath, on the other hand, were done as a demonstration of His love for them. Jesus put love before the law (the Mosaic Covenant); the Pharisees were condemning Him for showing love because of the law. God desires us to live in a manner that is all about displaying the love of Christ in everything we do and say.

God seeks people who "worship Him in spirit and in truth" as Jesus told the Samaritan woman at the well in John 4. People who do this love God and long to obey Him because they love Him, and for no other reason. Keeping the Sabbath because we love the Lord comes from the Holy Spirit connecting with our spirit and stirring up such love and devotion for Him. Our greatest desire comes from pleasing the Lord.

Seeing the Sabbath in this light makes it a joy and not a burden. Hence, if we keep it out of pure love for the Lord, not because it is the Law of Moses or the Moral Law, we will be blessed. We do not keep the Sabbath to earn something from God, but because we love God. We cannot earn what God has already freely given us.

25

Sabbath, Not Sadness

*E*mbracing the Sabbath should be seen as a true time of celebration and reflection. It is a moment when we should be especially grateful for all the Lord has done for us. The Sabbath was God's gift to the children of Israel to let them know it was okay to rest. As you may recall, they were under the oppressive bondage of Pharaoh, who made them work tirelessly. "So the Egyptians worked the people of Israel without mercy. They made their lives bitter, forcing them to mix mortar and make bricks and do all the work in the fields. They were ruthless in all their demands" (Exodus 1:13-14, NLT).

All the children of Israel knew was work. So, the Lord gave them the blessing of the Sabbath to let them know they could finally take time out to rest and reflect upon His goodness toward them. He wanted them to appreciate and celebrate where He had brought them from and what He had done for them.

God wants us to do the same thing today by happily and not haphazardly keeping the Sabbath. We have so much more to celebrate than even the children of Israel did because Jesus delivered us out of an even greater bondage than that of Egyptian oppression. Since Jesus died on the cross and saved us from our sin, we should have a joyful and rejoicing spirit when we honor Him, by taking time out from everything and everyone else on the Sabbath to joyously rest and meditate on His goodness, mercy, and love for us.

26

So What? Jesus Didn't Say It; He Did It

There are those who argue that since Jesus never actually said the Fourth Commandment for us to "Remember the Sabbath to keep it holy," that Christ's work on the cross did away with observing the Sabbath. Our best rebuttal to that false assertion can be found in these two profound words, "SO WHAT?"

So what if Christ doesn't mention it in the gospels? Our logical answer for this is, "Why mention what was still being practiced?" There was no reason for anyone, including Jesus or Paul, to make reference to keeping the Sabbath, as it was already part of their culture. The common practice to "Remember the Sabbath to keep it holy" was their way of life.

God the Father, Jesus, Paul and the other apostles, as well as the believers in the early church all honored the Sabbath.

There are other rituals, however, clearly addressed in the New Testament, that are unnecessary today.

Circumcision, for example, was one of those rituals that Paul pointed out was no longer needed. He said in Galatians 6:15 (NKJV), "For in Christ Jesus neither circumcision nor uncircumcision avails (means) anything, but a new creation." Some Jews were still convinced this Old Testament custom was necessary even for those who had become Christians. They missed the point, however, that this was not part of the Ten Commandments (Moral Law), but an aspect of keeping the Ceremonial Law, which Christ "blotted out," or "canceled," by "nailing it to His cross," as found in Colossians 2:14, which we discussed previously.

Even though circumcision is something we no longer have to do, you will not find anywhere in the Bible that keeping the Sabbath is no longer required, or that Jesus' death on the cross freed us from its observance. We are certain since Sabbath observance was such a staple of that day, and a strong and binding fabric of the Jewish nation, that if it were no longer necessary for us to do, then it would surely and clearly say so in the Bible. God still mandates that we, "Remember the Sabbath to keep it holy," which is exactly why Jesus, His disciples, and the early church regularly observed the Sabbath.

27

Stop Working On The Sabbath

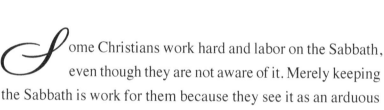

$\mathcal{S}$ome Christians work hard and labor on the Sabbath, even though they are not aware of it. Merely keeping the Sabbath is work for them because they see it as an arduous and laborious task. Since Sabbath keeping comes across as some "hard core" and "stressful" thing to do because of the self-denial it requires, many just do not honor it at all.

We were always told how difficult and boring keeping the Sabbath was. That's the way the Sabbath is presented by many, in such a bland and mundane manner that they would not make anyone who hears it interested in having anything to do with obeying the Lord by keeping His Sabbath.

We have to be and show forth excitement and enthusiasm when we tell others about the Sabbath. Look what God says about this in Isaiah 58:13 (NLT): "Keep the Sabbath day holy. Do not pursue your own interests on that day, *but enjoy the Sabbath and speak of it with delight* as the LORD's holy day.

Honor the Sabbath in everything you do on that day, and do not follow your own desires or talk idly."

28

Why Not Still Observe the Sabbath?

o you honestly think God no longer requires His children to give Him one day per week out of seven? Can you say in your heart that because Jesus died on the cross, we are no longer required to give God one total day of our uninterrupted time? You mean to tell us that if you say the observance of the Sabbath was under the Law, and since we are no longer under the Law (the Ceremonial Law) that we no longer have to spend one whole day in total dedication to God by remembering the Sabbath? Do you believe God would do away with this? We think you already know the answer to these questions, which is an unequivocal and emphatic "NO."

We have to believe that one of the biggest gripes the Lord has with us all is that we do not spend enough quality time with Him. We usually share our time with God, but not devote an entire day to Him without the daily distractions and interruptions of life. Anyone who believes that going to church in and of itself is "Remembering the Sabbath and keeping it holy" is sadly mistaken, and that goes for Saturday Sabbath observers, Sunday Sabbath observers, or any other day that Christians choose to observe the Sabbath and go to church.

Going to church denotes one aspect of observing the Sabbath, but it is only part of it and does not entirely constitute "Remembering the Sabbath," nor does it mean we are "keeping it holy." In our combined seventy-two years of attending church, we have heard these words repeatedly when asked which service people preferred to go to if their church had multiple services on the same day. They would always say, "Well I prefer to go to the early service because after that I'll have the rest of the day all to myself." Now think about it; is the Sabbath a day for us to have for ourselves or should it be a day, a holy day, that we totally give to the Lord?

Section 3

Life in the Lord of the Sabbath

This is the part of the book that gives us the most excitement! In this section, we have the opportunity to share ways we can enjoy Jesus as we celebrate the Sabbath. We will demonstrate how seeing Jesus as the Lord of the Sabbath and keeping Him at the center of your Sabbath experience can enrich your life with Him and your relationships with others.

29

The Sabbath, The Holiest Day of Them All, PERIOD

Let us begin with the Christian holidays that bring us together as family and friends. Good Friday, Resurrection Sunday (Easter), and Christmas are all considered "High Holy Days" on the Christian calendar. While they do emphasize Christ's birth, life, death, and resurrection here on earth, highlighting these days as high and holy was designated by man, not by the Lord.

There is only one day that God Himself deemed as holy: the Sabbath, even though we know we are required to live holy each and every day. So while we have great respect and reverence for our manmade Christian holy days, as we continue to honor the Lord and reflect on what He has done, we esteem and celebrate the Sabbath on an even greater and higher level because it is the only day God quotes in His Word as being holy. Because of that, we believe the Sabbath is the holiest day of all, PERIOD!

30

The Sabbath is not Just a DAY; it is a WAY

*O*ur mindset and focus for keeping the Sabbath must be viewed as something more than just taking time out to cease, stop, and resist the urge to work on that particular day. For the child of God, observing the Sabbath must be seen as not just a routine, ritual, or habit. We must embrace the Sabbath and live it out as our way of life. This requires what we call "A Sabbath Mentality."

A Sabbath Mentality: Please, Don't Appease

Remembering the Sabbath and keeping it holy means we can keep it holy only according to God's standards, not our own. We cannot give Him part of the Sabbath and do what we want rest of the day.

Some, however, will say, "Well at least I am giving God some of my time on the Sabbath because I am going to church," when they're really doing this as a means of appeasing God. We must keep in mind, however, that God has never asked us or wants us to appease Him; rather, He *requires* that we please Him. Hebrews 11:6 (KJV) states, "But without faith [it is] impossible to please [him] (God)."

You may be surprised to know that some people who keep the Sabbath do not have a Sabbath mentality. Let us explore what God says a "Sabbath Mentality" is.

Jesus is Still Lord of the Sabbath

We make the constant effort to reinforce that Jesus is Lord of the Sabbath. He is the fiber and the root of the Sabbath. That has not changed. We are purposely and consistently keeping this point foremost in our minds because it is so easy to become consumed with the responsibility of working to keep the Sabbath.

In one of Jesus' discourses with the Pharisees, we see them focused on the aspects of keeping the Sabbath, which Moses put in place. In Matthew 12:1-3, they point out the fact that the disciples were picking heads of grain to eat, which the Mosaic Law refers to as work, unlawful to do on the Sabbath. Jesus, however, saw this act as a necessity because the disciples were hungry.

Jesus responded to the Pharisees by saying that "God desires mercy, not sacrifice," indicating the importance of the position of one's heart rather than one's actions. Even though the Pharisees were diligently obeying the Mosaic Law, the position of their hearts was not humble regarding the true things of God. Because of this, they could not see the importance of relationship over ritual regarding the Sabbath. This is not evidence of a "Sabbath Mentality."

Jesus concludes His conversation with them by saying in verse 8, "For I, the Son of Man, is Lord of the Sabbath," declaring Himself the focal point, the center, the very core and the essence of the Sabbath. By doing this, He shows the Sabbath is nothing without Him. We can prepare very well for the Sabbath. We can organize various activities for this holy day. We can even lead a Sabbath day service, but if the position of our hearts is not humble toward Jesus by making Him the principle reason for our Sabbath celebration, we are not keeping Him as Lord of the Sabbath.

31

What Does God Say We Should Not Do During the Sabbath?

$\mathscr{M}$any of us are familiar with the various things we cannot do during the Sabbath, according to the Mosaic Law. But the Lord also has a list of things we are not to do on this holy day of the week. You can find it in Isaiah 58:13-14 (NIV):

> "If you keep your feet from breaking the Sabbath
> and from doing as you please on my holy day,
> if you call the Sabbath a delight and the LORD's
> holy day honorable, and if you honor it by not
> going your own way and not doing as you please
> or speaking idle words, then you will find your
> joy in the LORD, and I will cause you to ride in
> triumph on the heights of the land and to feast

on the inheritance of your father Jacob." For the mouth of the LORD has spoken.

Can you sense from the solemn tone of these Scriptures how serious the Lord is about the Sabbath and keeping it holy? It is obviously extremely important to Him. Let's examine the things He instructs us not to do.

"Doing Your Own Pleasure"

Doing your own pleasure on God's holy day is discouraged. These would be any activities that take your concentration away from God, including acts that bring you particular joy as it relates to your own personality, and all other areas of your life that are not particular responsibilities, but undertakings that may cause enjoyment to you as an individual, such as watching the game, going shopping, or doing other things that take your attention away from Jesus and put the focus on you alone. Instead, we should be engaged in activities that cause us to think about Jesus and His creation so that we remember Jesus and keep the day holy. We are to trust in the Lord to help us keep His will and do His pleasure during the day. In doing so, we will be giving God the glory.

"Not Doing Our Own Way(s)"

Job 23:11 (NIV) says, "My feet have closely followed His steps; I have kept to his way without turning aside." In this verse, Job is emphasizing not doing our own ways. This refers to all the responsibilities we have during the week, trying to satisfy our personal goals and aspirations. These include working on our personal accomplishments and singular successes. Instead we are to focus on the Lord and remember Him, not ourselves, on this day.

"Not Speaking Our Own Words"

Not speaking our own words is a difficult facet of keeping the Sabbath. It involves not speaking words of discouragement; complaints; criticism; lies; negativity; doubt; and a great deal of other words, information, or opinions that do not glorify God. For some of us, this is difficult because these words are so much a part of our everyday language. Some of us are not even aware that we are speaking this way and need to be in deep prayer about this part of the list because our words are important to the Lord. Psalm 19:14 (KJV) tells us, "Let the words of my mouth, and the meditation of my heart, be acceptable in thy sight, O LORD, my strength, and my redeemer." This shows us the Lord is listening to our words and they are significant, especially during the Sabbath.

One must admit this is a more meaningful, constructive, and spiritual list than the one found in the Mosaic Law, as it relates to keeping the Sabbath, because the heart and mind of a person must be actively involved in keeping the Sabbath holy. This is the "Sabbath Mentality," to which we refer as we please Jesus instead of appeasing Him. In this way, we can maintain a "Sabbath Mentality," and be delighted about keeping the Sabbath all the more, which brings us closer to the Lord Jesus.

The most wonderful part of this list is that we know God Himself established it. The end of the Scripture states, "The mouth of the LORD has spoken." Notice the word "LORD" is in all capital letters, which signifies that Jehovah, God, the Creator, is He who speaks. The Creator desires us to reflect on His creation during the Sabbath; therefore, this list should be taken as seriously as God takes it. This means we should pray to stay away from the activities on this list because it will not produce a "Sabbath Mentality."

32

How to Keep JESUS in the Sabbath

*N*ow, let's explore the "Sabbath Mentality" as it relates to keeping Jesus the primary focus of the day. Most Christians call Sunday the Sabbath and believe if they go to church in the morning, they have fulfilled their obligation of remembering the Sabbath and keeping it holy. Not only have they neglected to remember the Sabbath, which is Saturday, but they have also neglected to keep it holy because they do whatever they want after leaving church. This is not true remembrance or holy observance of the Sabbath because they are making themselves and their desires the center of their Sabbath experience instead of Jesus. They are giving Jesus only a fraction of the day. This is not keeping Jesus in the Sabbath.

We have also found that some Saturday Sabbath observers remember the day, but do not keep it holy, as their minds may not be on Jesus but on the responsibilities that are to come. Or they may argue with their loved ones. Or they may exhibit impatience or negative attitudes during the day. Many Sunday Christians do this as well. Again, they are focused on their feelings or other aspects of their lives, which takes their minds off Jesus. This too is not keeping Jesus in the Sabbath or doing anything to promote a "Sabbath Mentality."

The Importance of Time in Relationships

The more time we spend with God, the more we become like Him, the more He shows us the direction He has for us, and the more joy we have. Psalm 16:11 (NKJV) says, "You will show me the path of life; In Your presence [is] fullness of joy; At Your right hand [are] pleasures forevermore." Also, the more time we spend with God, the closer we get to Him, and the closer He gets to us. James 4:8 (KJV) says, "Draw nigh (near) to God, and he will draw nigh (near) to you." The NLT puts it this way, "Come close to God, and God will come close to you."

Keeping the Sabbath Is Tithing Our Time

Time is truly of the essence. We are living in a society where everyone is so busy and weary all the time. A week is composed of seven days, or 168 hours. If you work forty hours a week, that leaves 128 hours left for ourselves. The average person sleeps about eight hours a day, which totals fifty-six hours for the week. This leaves us only seventy-two hours left for ourselves, and even then, about half that time is devoted to family and household obligations. That would then leave approximately thirty-six hours (a day and a half) left for ourselves.

Now "church time" is the allotted time the average Christian spends in church during the week. The average service last about two hours. We may also attend a weeknight prayer meeting or Bible study, which lasts about an hour and a half. This leaves us with approximately thirty-two and a half hours for ourselves, or one full twenty-four-hour day, plus an additional eight and a half hours of "me time."

It is in our best interest to take a Sabbath rest, or twenty-four hours. That would still leave us with eight and a half hours left for ourselves. Most of us sleep about eight hours on the Sabbath. So, after deducting those eight hours, we spend only about sixteen of the twenty-four hours in the day.

We equate keeping the Sabbath to "tithing our time" to God. If we divide the 168 hours that make up the week, by ten, which is the 10 percent the Lord asks us to give Him as a tithe, it equals 16.8 hours. This is approximately the amount of time we give God when we engage in taking the Sabbath rest.

Throughout scripture, the Lord blesses those who give what is due Him, which is not only a tithe of our finances, but of our time. When the Lord tells us in Malachi 3:10 (NKJV), "Bring all the tithes into the storehouse, that there may be food in my house, and try me now in this says the LORD of host, if I will not open for you the windows of Heaven and pour out for you such blessing that there will not be room enough to receive it," although the Scripture is referring to our finances, we can also apply this principle to the time that God requires us to spend with Him. Everyone should be willing to give the Lord a tithe (16.8 hours) of their time, out of their seven-day week. Isn't He worth that and more?

Routine, Ritual, or Relationship?

When we keep the Sabbath out of love for God, because of our relationship with Christ, we give more to Him and get more from Him than if we do it because it is a routine or a ritual.

We must truly keep the Fourth Commandment to honor, obey, and enhance our relationship with our God, who made the day and blessed us to be alive to see it. The more seriously we take observing the Sabbath, the deeper our relationship will be with the Lord.

The Lord requires us to observe the Sabbath because He desires to be intimate with us, not to intimidate us. God does not want any of us to feel like He is forcing us to keep the Sabbath out of sheer compulsion. On the contrary, He definitely wants us to keep it because we love Him. 1 John 4:19 (KJV) says, "We love Him, because he first loved us."

We also need to be aware that the Sabbath was given to us as a "good and perfect gift" from God. Scripture make it clear that, "Every good and perfect gift is from above, coming down from the Father of lights" (James 1:17, NLT). The Lord gave us this precious gift for an important reason, which is found in Ezekiel 20:12 (KJV): "Moreover also I gave them my Sabbaths, to be a sign between me and them, that they might know that I am the Lord that sanctify them."

The Lord makes it quite clear that the Sabbath was given to us as a sign of His relationship with us. Ezekiel 20:20 in the New English Translation (NET) says, "I also gave them my Sabbaths as a reminder of our relationship, so that they would know that I, the Lord, sanctify them." The Sabbath is all about "relationship." Unfortunately, some people in Scripture were attempting to turn the Sabbath into a religious ritual experience that encompassed manmade rules and regulations, instead of using the day to focus on their relationship with God.

The Pharisees, for example, repeatedly accused Jesus and His disciples of breaking the Sabbath (Matthew 12:1-8, Mark 2:23-28, Mark 3:1-6, Luke 6:1-11, Luke 13:10-16). As you examine these passages closely, you will see that the Pharisees had no idea the Sabbath had anything to do with a "relationship" with God and with others as well. Instead they relegated the Sabbath to just following the "ritualistic practices" they instituted, without understanding the aspect of "relationship."

The Pharisees were still following the old system that was not open to embracing the new and living way Jesus presented to them. Jesus wanted them to move from just keeping numerous rituals to having a meaningful relationship with Him and with other people. But instead they chose to keep the rituals rather than embracing God's gift to them.

Approach is Everything

Do not look forward to the end of the Sabbath more than you do the beginning. Some people spend more time counting down to the end of the Sabbath than they do embracing the entire experience. But the way we prepare for the Sabbath is crucial to how we will observe it. What we do leading up to it determines the effectiveness it will have in our lives. The Lord says in Proverbs 16:3 (NIV), "Commit to the Lord whatever you do, and he will establish your plans." This is true not only for anything we do in life, but also for the Sabbath. In our first few weeks of keeping the Sabbath, we found it difficult to manage our time in order to be prepared for it at sundown on Friday. We rushed to have all our work done, including cooking, cleaning, responding to emails, shopping, and various other activities. Many times, we would complete everything just before sundown. This made us extremely uncomfortable, as we were flustered when the Sabbath came in. It was our desire to be calm in meeting the Sabbath. We discussed the matter together and agreed we must organize our time more efficiently.

We decided not to wait until Friday to attend to the things we would usually do on Saturday. Instead, we decided to do them during the week. This took a great deal of organization skills. Fortunately, the Lord blessed us with a specific Word about preparing for the Sabbath. He said, "Preparation for the Sabbath begins sundown, Saturdays."

At that point, every Saturday at sundown, we would take small steps toward preparing for the Sabbath. By sundown on

Fridays, we were completely prepared for the Sabbath, so we were not overwhelmed when the Sabbath began. Instead, we were calm and patiently waiting its arrival.

Now we find ourselves rejoicing and worshipping the Lord long before sundown on Fridays, and we have praised the Lord for helping us understand the Sabbath is not something we can prepare for haphazardly, as an afterthought. On the contrary, the Lord wishes us to look forward to the Sabbath rest, not worry about work that needs to be done.

33

Eight Benefits of Observing the Sabbath

*M*any people think of keeping the Sabbath as a litany of things they can and cannot do. So they rush to get these things done before the Sabbath begins, and watch the clock in anticipation for the Sabbath to end so they can resume their own business.

Unfortunately, their perception of this Holy Day does little to enhance their relationship with Jesus. This is why we will now examine eight benefits of observing the Sabbath. Each benefit is supported by the Word of God and focuses on helping your walk with Jesus to flourish. By understanding these eight benefits, you will begin to look forward to the Sabbath, resulting in a relationship with the Lord Jesus that will become deeper and more mature.

Joy

Joy is a characteristic of Christian living that is sometimes obscured by our daily responsibilities, disappointments, and personal trials. In Isaiah 58:13-14, we find that joy is a result of keeping the Sabbath. By seeing the Sabbath as a chance to hear from the Lord and focus on His glory, joy will eventually develop as a byproduct of changing your outlook of the Sabbath and overflow into your daily life and activities. As a result, you will be consistently spending a significant amount of time with Jesus. Nehemiah 8:10 (KJV) says, "The joy of the Lord is your strength."

An Intensifying Daily Devotion Time

During the Sabbath, we should be engaged in spiritual principles that elevate our walks with the Lord Jesus the entire day. During this time, our hearts should be open to Him, making it easier for us to sense His presence. The Lord Jesus says it best in John 15:1-5 (ESV):

> I am the true vine, and my Father is the vinedresser. Every branch in me that does not bear fruit he takes away, and every branch that does bear fruit he prunes, that it may bear more fruit. Already you are clean because of the word that I have spoken to you. Abide in me, and I in you. As the branch cannot bear fruit by itself, unless

it abides in the vine, neither can you, unless you abide in me. I am the vine; you are the branches. Whoever abides in me and I in him, he it is that bears much fruit, for apart from me you can do nothing.

Abiding in Jesus, which means enjoying close fellowship with Him daily, adds to our growth in the Lord. We have found this to be especially true when we do this on the Sabbath. We believe that you, too, will find abiding in Jesus so exhilarating that it will spill over into your daily devotional times, making them more meaningful and delightful.

A Toned Spiritual Ear

With a more intensifying daily devotional time, you will be surprised at how your spiritual ear will become more tuned to God's voice for knowing His will in your life. John 10:27 (KJV) says, "My sheep hear my voice, and I know them, and they follow me." Reading God's Holy Word regularly, and with prayer and humility, will make you more conscious of God's voice. John 15:15 (NIV) says, "I no longer call you servants, because a servant does not know his master's business. Instead, I have called you friends, for everything that I learned from my Father I have made known to you."

You will begin to see theses Scriptures manifest in your consistent one-on-one time with the Lord when you will hear His plans and desires for your life. Your ear will become more tuned to hearing His voice and understanding His Word, causing your relationship with Him to flourish. Such a benefit finds its roots in "Remembering the Sabbath and keeping it holy."

Obtaining Great Honor

Isaiah 58:14 (NIV) says, "the Lord will give us great honor" when we keep the Sabbath as prescribed in verse 13. The idea of obtaining greater honor is very appealing in the natural sense. We all want to have the honor and respect of our loved ones, peers, and superiors, but obtaining great honor with the Lord Jesus is a benefit far greater than that of any human being that will incur us favor with both God and man. We will have His blessings and His approval of all that we do for His glory.

Success in Our Endeavors

As we are experiencing a closer walk with the Lord due to the blessings of keeping the Sabbath, we can expect success in our endeavors. Psalm 37:4 (NIV) says, "Take delight in the LORD, and he will give you the desires of your heart." The Lord's desires will become our desires as a consequence of spending quality time with Him; therefore, the Lord will unquestionably grant His own petition and His will for our lives. Then His will and ours will become impeccably one.

Recalling Isaiah 58:14, keeping the Sabbath will give us an added aspect to our successful living. This verse states that when we keep the Sabbath, "we will ride upon the high places of the earth." This provides an awesome thought. We can find a wonderful reward and great fulfillment in our endeavors as a result of "Remembering the Sabbath and keeping it holy."

The Inheritance of Jacob

Isaiah 58:14 also states that a consequence of keeping the Sabbath is obtaining the "Inheritance of Jacob." According to the Old Testament, the "Inheritance of Jacob" refers to entering into and possessing the land promised to Abraham. It was a land with great renumerations. In our case, the "Inheritance of Jacob," or the "Promised Land" signifies everlasting life, which begins now. Just as God's people enjoyed the blessings of the "Promised Land," we can enjoy the advantages of eternal life by living an abundant life now.

Natural Rest

The blessing of rest that comes from keeping the Sabbath is not only spiritual, but physical. When we are single-minded about keeping the Sabbath, we can be confident that we are in God's will and in His care. So we do not need to be concerned with our weekly responsibilities during the Sabbath because God will keep them all in His care. This natural rest is clearly emphasized in Exodus 20:9-10 (NIV):

> Six days you shall labor and do all your work,
> but the seventh day is a sabbath to the LORD

your God. On it you shall not do any work, neither you, nor your son or daughter, nor your
male or female servant, nor your animals, nor
any foreigner residing in your towns.

Taking a day away from natural work has even greater
advantages. This natural rest is the only significant rest many
of us experience after a long week. Taking time not to work,
worry, or complain, therefore, can have enormous benefits for
our bodies.

Perfect Peace

Perfect peace during the Sabbath results from focusing
solely on Jesus, giving our minds rest and peace from our own
struggles and challenges that are part of daily living. Isaiah
26:3 (KJV) says, "thou wilt keep him in perfect peace, whose
mind is stayed on thee: because he trusteth in thee." This perfect peace is a wonderful way to live life in such a stressful,
high-paced society.

34

Keeping the Sabbath Can Enhance Our Relationships

*R*elationships are important to God, and therefore should be important to us. After all, God did give His Son to bring us into a right relationship with Him so we can have everlasting life. We must remember that each individual in a relationship provides a weighty contribution to its union as stated in Ephesians 4:16-17 (KJV):

> But speaking the truth in love, may grow up into
> him in all things, which is the head, even Christ:
> From whom the whole body fitly joined together
> and compacted by that which every joint sup-
> plieth, according to the effectual working in the
> measure of every part, maketh increase of the
> body unto the edifying of itself in love.

In short, uniting with others in a God-glorifying way will increase our Sabbath experience because loved ones are taking an active part in making it more meaningful.

Spending Quality Time Growing Together Spiritually

Many of us are too busy to spend a significant amount of time with our families during the week. Parents are busy working and are too tired to make a connection with their children. Husbands are too exhausted at night to have deep conversations with their wives. The Sabbath gives us the freedom to spend quality time with our families and loved ones. It is a beautiful time to examine the glorious things God has done in your lives that week. This gives us a chance to encourage each other in the Lord, share concerns, and pray together.

The Sabbath can be also used to reconnect weekly with those members of the church we have not seen in a while. The body of Christ needs constant assembling to strengthen each joint. "Every joint supplieth" and consequently needs nurturing, encouragement, and love to become robust. This comes from pouring into each other's lives in ways that are positive, helpful, and affirmative.

We can now see how remembering the Sabbath and keeping it holy can help grow more lasting and loving relationships. Resting from our labors one day a week gives us added time to glorify Him in our relationships with others.

Do not Put the Sabbath Before the People; Put the People Before the Sabbath

We should never put the Sabbath before relationships with people. In putting the "idea" of keeping the Sabbath before our relationships with family and friends, we miss a very important part of what Jesus is saying to the Pharisees in Matthew 12:7-8 (NIV): "If only you had known the meaning of 'I desire mercy, not sacrifice,' you would not have condemned the innocent. For the Son on Man is Lord of the Sabbath."

Relationships can be irreparably damaged when we put the rituals of a day before relationships. This is the sacrifice we make when we put the Sabbath before people. But God desires the merciful acts of loving, listening, praying together, sharing, visiting, and having heart-to-heart communication with each other. This can be done in creative ways on the Sabbath, and Jesus will be glorified in the process. In doing so, we are not only keeping our relationships healthy and holy, but we are growing closer to each other as we grow closer to the Lord on His holy day.

Do not Wait Until the Sabbath to "Iron Things Out"

While even in the most loving relationships it's natural to be at odds at times, the Sabbath is not the time to "iron" those issues out. On the contrary, Matthew 18:15 (NLT) says, "If another believer sins against you, go privately and point out the offense. When the other person listens and confesses it, you have won that person back." The Lord also tells us in Ephesians 4:26-27 (NIV) precisely when to reconcile with those who have offended us: "In your anger do not sin: Do not let the sun go down while you are still angry, and do not give the devil a foothold."

It is important, therefore, to reconcile with our loved ones as soon as possible. Being at odds with them can impede our Sabbath celebration because it takes the focus off Jesus and puts it on the conflict. This kind of attitude does nothing to give glory to the Lord on His holy day. In fact, it brings an element of unholiness to the Sabbath. So, please, let us "iron out" our conflicts before the Sabbath begins. You will see how God blesses the day as you worship Him, knowing you are in fellowship with the people in your life.

35

Effective Ways to Use Your Time During the Sabbath

*W*hile some find it difficult to use their time effectively during the Sabbath, there are many creative ways to spend this holy day if you are organized and innovative. In fact, the Lord has given us an inspiring way to divide our time during the Sabbath. Following are five areas of a Christian's spiritual life that can be deeply affected by the Sabbath.

Spending Private Time with the Lord

Spending private time with the Lord should be your primary worship. Psalm 91:1 (NIV) shows the glorious results of this intimate experience: "Whoever dwells in the shelter of the Most High will rest in the shadow of the Almighty." This is also a time to receive a personal Word from the Lord that will surely edify you and make your life flourish. Having alone time with Him is one of our favorite parts of the Sabbath experience because it builds our personal walks with Christ.

Spending Time in Church (Corporate Worship)

Going to the synagogue was a regular practice of Jesus and God's people during the Sabbath, as demonstrated in Luke 4:16 (NLT): "When he came to the village of Nazareth, his boyhood home, he went as usual to the synagogue on the Sabbath and stood up to read the Scriptures." We strongly suggest, therefore, that this practice be maintained. Attending church is a time to worship the Lord, receive a weekly encouraging Word, and interact with Christians you have not seen during the week.

Keep in mind, however, that this activity should not be your primary source of worship or the primary way you hear from the Lord. You should be worshipping God and receiving a personal Word from Him during your daily devotional times. Corporate worship should be a supplement to your regular devotional time, not a substitute for it.

Spending Time with the Saints

Enjoying the joys and triumphs of the week with other believers, even outside of church, is an excellent way to enjoy the Sabbath. Hebrews 10:25 (ESV) encourages us to do this by, "Not neglecting to meet together, as is the habit of some, but encouraging one another, and all the more as you see the Day drawing near."

Some are ill or unable to make a Sabbath service for various reasons, but this should not deter us from coming together to share prayer concerns and worship together. This not only honors the Sabbath, but it builds your relationship with others in a way that pleases God.

Spending Time with Family Members

During our busy lives, we sometimes miss the subtle things that may be occurring with our spouses, children, parents, and extended family. Using the Sabbath to discuss life in the Lord will update us on what God is doing in the lives of our families and give us a chance to provide our own updates as well so we can receive support and encouragement as well as give it. 1 Timothy 5:8 (ESV) says it best: "But if anyone does not provide for his relatives, and especially for members of his household, he has denied the faith and is worse than an unbeliever."

In this statement, the Lord shows us the high value He places on relationships. "Providing for one's relatives" not only pertains to material needs, but to our families' emotional and spiritual needs as well. God has given us the Sabbath to help nurture this rapport. Specifically…

Spend Time with Your Spouse

Communication is mandatory for couples to meet the obligations of their lives. Genesis 2:18 (NIV) illustrates the importance of maintaining healthy communication with our spouses: "The LORD God said, "It is not good for the man to be alone. I will make a helper suitable for him." We urge spouses to spend more quality one-one-one time with each other during the Sabbath to discuss what the Lord is doing in your marriage. Talk about where you are in your lives together and where you feel the Lord is leading you as a couple.

Spend Time with Your Children

Using the Sabbath to grow closer to your children is a blessing in which you will find many benefits. During the week, several things occur in our children's lives, especially in their formative (adolescent) years. They have questions, they have challenges, and they have concerns. They need your undivided attention to help them move from one phase of their lives to another, which happens very quickly.

The Sabbath is an opportune time to connect your hearts with your children's. You and the Lord can assist them in their growth and development in a valuable way by spending an allotted family time together.

36

Activities To Do on the Sabbath

*M*any people are frustrated by all the things they cannot do on the Sabbath. There are many exciting and fun things you can do, however, that have nothing whatsoever to do with work. These activities even have the added benefits of fellowshipping with family and friends while lifting up the name of Jesus, prompting you to keep Him in your heart during your time together. These activities are as follows:

1. Christian karaoke gives you the opportunity to sing songs that magnify the Lord.
2. Bible Trivia helps you realize how much you know about God's Word and learn things you do not know.
3. Memorizing the books of the Bible in order helps you learn to find them quickly.

4. "Name that Bible Character" assists you in under-standing the various people in God's Word and the important contributions they made.

5. Having relaxing in-home fellowship events that encourage unity with family and friends and promote edification in their walks with Christ.

6. Enjoying a good meal together is always a great way to bond and connect our hearts with others. This time can be used to honor the relationships you have created with each other, remembering that God has united you, and that He will maintain your relationships as you keep Him in the center of them.

Children involved in your Sabbath activities should have a major part in deciding how they should be carried out. This helps them feel as though they're contributing not only to the activities but to the family unit as a whole.

37

Which Do You Love More,
The Sign or the Savior?

s we already mentioned, some exalt the Sabbath higher than they do Jesus, the God who made the day itself. We believe any Christian who does this has made the Sabbath into an image of idolatry, placing it before "Jesus" Himself.

The Sabbath serves as the Lord's sign to His children. Exodus 31:13 (KJV) says, "Speak thou also unto the children of Israel, saying, Verily my sabbaths ye shall keep: for it [is] a sign between me and you throughout your generations; that [ye] may know that I [am] the LORD that doth sanctify you."

The word *sign* is defined as "a token, indication, or any object, action, event, or pattern that conveys a meaning or a notice; or bears a name, direction, warning, or advertisement, that is displayed or posted for public view." Signs are designed to show us how to get to places we desire to go. The Sabbath is the sign, and Jesus is the destination we should want to get to. He is the one who the sign, the Sabbath, points to. If we stop at the sign (the Sabbath) and put it above our ultimate destination (Jesus), we will never get to Him.

Some observe signs while others do not. But the main reason we get lost, fail in our endeavors, or miss out on reaching a desired destination in life is because we do not follow signs. Paying attention to signs is imperative for everyone to do; just keep in mind that worship is reserved only for our Lord Jesus Christ, who says in Luke 4:8 (KJV), "Thou shalt worship the Lord thy God, and him only shalt thou serve." So make sure you are not stopping at the sign; make sure you get to the Savior, Jesus, the Lord of the Sabbath.

Exodus 31:13 also reveals God's purpose for the Sabbath, which is a "sign between Him and us," and how long the "sign of the Sabbath" lasts: "throughout your generations [plural]." This is a clear indication that God intends for us to partake in honoring His Sabbath rest throughout our lifetimes and beyond. Keeping the Sabbath must be passed down to our "generations" to come, without end.

38

The Fulfillment of Observing the Sabbath, Oneness with God

*T*he relationship between God and man is the closest relationship a human being can experience. While we have prayerfully shared the benefits of "Remembering the day and keeping it holy," the true fulfillment of the observance comes from being one with the Lord for the entire day, spending the whole day in His glory.

Because of our busy lives, many of us are unable to spend a great amount of time experiencing this oneness during the week. But during the Sabbath, we have the liberty to pour our thoughts into the things of God, a freedom God gives us in a way that we do not have during the week. We are to use this time, therefore, to enjoy our union with Jesus.

In becoming one with God, we are experiencing the fulfillment of the goal of the Sabbath. 1 Corinthians 6:17 (NIV) says, "But whoever is united with the Lord is one with him in spirit." Uniting with Jesus on the Sabbath is one of the greatest ways God brings us together with Him. As we experience the fullness of His presence, we are experiencing the fulfillment of what the Lord designated this holy day to be, a time of resting, being one with Him, and enjoying His creation.

39

Sharing this Information

*W*e must "keep the Sabbath holy," but not keep the Sabbath to ourselves. We are blessed when we keep the Sabbath and we should want others to partake in the rest that comes with observing it. Isaiah 56:2 (NLT) gives us an incentive to share the beauty of the Sabbath with others: "Blessed are all those who are careful to do this. Blessed are those who honor my Sabbath days of rest and keep themselves from doing wrong." By sharing it, we keep others from being out of God's will and encourage them to experience the blessings of devoting one day to Him.

Conversation Not Confrontation

We recall how information about the Sabbath was given to us, by Saturday Sabbath observers. Often times, the information was presented in a way that was forced and oppositional.

This did nothing to warm our hearts toward the information. On the contrary, it made us "dig in our heels" more firmly. Thus, many of our discussions became confrontational because we were not open to hearing any of the valid, legitimate points being made in support of it. But by studying the Word, the Lord opened our hearts and enlightened our understanding.

He taught us a great deal about presenting this knowledge to people in a way that is palatable and comprehensive. We have discovered a conversation about the Sabbath is more effective than a confrontation, which can cause dissension. Ephesians 4:15-16 (KJV) supports sharing the truth about the Sabbath in love:

> But speaking the truth in love, may grow up into him in all things, which is the head, even Christ: From whom the whole body fitly joined together and compacted by that which every joint sup-plieth, according to the effectual working in the measure of every part, maketh increase of the body unto the edifying of itself in love.

In light of this, we would like to share the steps to help you share your Sabbath experiences with others and reasons for keeping it when the Lord leads you to do so. Following these steps has opened the conversation for more exploration.

Explore Your Reasons for Sharing The Sabbath

First, examine your reasons for wanting to share the information about the Sabbath. If we are not coming from a pure, God-glorifying centered place, then we will not be successful in sharing the Sabbath. But if we are coming from a position of love for the Lord Jesus, and are presenting the information about observing the Sabbath out of genuine concern for mankind and its relationship with God, then Jesus will be pleased with our efforts.

Allow Sufficient Time to Share

The time in which you speak to a person about the Sabbath is important. Do not choose a time when you will have to rush the conversation. You or the person with whom you are speaking should not be busy with other things that demand attention, such as work, children, or extra responsibilities. Make the conversation as casual as possible, even if you have to schedule a time to meet. Because the information is spiritual, the conversation should be unhurried and unpressured.

Choose a Place Conducive to Natural Sharing

Choose a place that is comfortable for both of you. If you or the person with whom you are speaking does not want the conversation overheard, talk in a quiet place where you can have privacy.

The atmosphere should be one of peace, love, and comfort. It should be relaxed, not strained, noisy, or distracting. If the atmosphere is not conducive to an easy-going conversation, then wait for a time when it is more tranquil and information can flow freely.

Open with, "What Does the Sabbath Mean to You?"

We start our conversations with this question. This is an open-ended question that will tell you how much the person to whom you are speaking knows about the Sabbath. Once you discover this, you will be able to determine how much to share with that person. Depending on the content of the conversation, following are some other open-ended questions to consider asking:

- Why do you think it is no longer important or needed to keep the Sabbath?
- Where does the Bible say we no longer have keep it?
- Do you believe by keeping the Sabbath you are breaking God's Law?
- Do you believe Christ's death on the cross meant we should no longer observe the Sabbath?
- Do you believe the Lord no longer requires His children to dedicate and spend 24 (16) hours with Him, which is less than one day out of a seven-day week?

Be Mindful of Your Body Language

Your posture, hand movements, facial expressions, and eye contact can all make the person to whom you are speaking feel secure or insecure. So, be alert and maintain an expression of interest in what the person is saying. This means maintaining eye contact. Also, do not interrupt the person when he or she is speaking or answering a question you have posed.

Keep a Relationship with Jesus at the Heart of the Conversation

Jesus is the Lord of the Sabbath, so a relationship with Him is essential. Whether you agree about observing the Sabbath or not, both of you need to remain connected by the love you have for the Lord. Do not let a disagreement about the Sabbath divide you from the people with whom you are sharing. Hence, Jesus must be the common factor among us.

Provide Follow Up That is Natural

Follow up should be as natural as the initial conversation. You do not have to call the person back to see if they have thought about what you have said about Sabbath observance. If you happen to see that person, you may want to (very casually) ask if they have given the discussion any thought or prayer. Do not pressure anyone. Remember the Sabbath is a gift from the

Lord. Although it is freely given, it may not be openly received, so please respect other people's decisions.

Plant a Seed and Pray for Growth

When sharing the Sabbath, remember the assignment is two-fold. First, plant a seed by giving people the information of the glorious Sabbath. The conversation about the aspects of the Sabbath is the seed we plant by having a loving, honest dialog, referring people to the Scriptures to support your statements.

Second, pray for God to give the increase. Ask the Lord to nurture the seed and make it grow into something beautiful and glorifying to Him. He did it for you and He will do it for others. The Lord says in 1 Corinthians 3:6-9 (NIV):

> I planted the seed, Apollos watered it, but God has been making it grow. So neither the one who plants nor the one who waters is anything, but only God, who makes things grow. The one who plants and the one who waters have one purpose, and they will each be rewarded according to their own labor. For we are co-workers in God's service; you are God's field, God's building.

Remember, you are conversing with people about the Sabbath, not confronting them. The idea is to have a free-flowing exchange of information, where both of you can learn and grow from the points shared in the dialogue. Most importantly, the love of Jesus must remain the eternal bond between you.

40

Sabbath Observance, From Revelation to Revolution

*W*e believe the message of the Sabbath is life changing and we are committed to sharing it with the world. Since the Lord has enlightened us to celebrating the seventh day, He has taken us from one revelation to another regarding its various aspects and benefits. Each revelation has lifted Jesus higher as Lord of the Sabbath.

Because this knowledge is not clearly articulated in the churches that have services on Sunday, we have been commissioned by the Lord to share this information with them. We are certain that when this powerful message is understood, the knowledge will be embraced and celebrated in these churches. As a result, many will grow, be healed, and thrive in all they do because they are keeping the Sabbath God's way. Isaiah 58:14 (KJV) bests describes the rewards of keeping the Sabbath:

"then shalt thou delight thyself in the Lord; and I will cause thee to ride upon the high places of the earth, and feed thee with the heritage of Jacob thy father: for the mouth of the Lord hath spoken it."

Conclusion

The Salvation Message

In exposing the truth about why we should still observe the Sabbath on the seventh day, we have demonstrated the true "savviness" of the Sabbath. In doing so, we will conclude the book the same way we began it, with the message of salvation. Jesus is the Lord of the Sabbath and therefore must be acknowledged as such. He said in John 3:7 (KJV), "Marvel not that I said unto thee, Ye must be born again." This must be done to even acknowledge Him as "Lord of the Sabbath."

If you are not born again, we take this time to introduce Jesus Christ to you. He has redeemed your soul from the gates of hell and has made a home for you in heaven. You have everlasting life, which begins now, if you accept Him as your Lord. You will find an unlimited source of love, patience, and kindness in your relationship with Jesus that you will never find in any human being. He will not fail you.

If you have received Him, begin the first day of the rest of your life with Jesus today. Find continued celebration and joy in keeping the Sabbath day holy. Allow these Sabbath principles to enrich your relationship with Him and others. We guarantee that your life will never be the same. You will "ride on the high places of the earth," as you "Remember the Sabbath and keep it holy." Amen.

References

Batchelor, D. (2011). Seven facts about the 7th day. Amazing Facts. Retrieved from https://www.amazingfacts.org

Catholic Church (1994). The Catechism of the Catholic Church Section 2, Article 3. Document on Church Doctrine. Roman Catholic Church

Crews, J. (2007). Feast days & sabbaths—Are they still binding? Retrieved from https://www.amazingfacts.org

https://www.dictionary.com

Gibbon, E. (1960). The History of the Decline and Fall of the Roman Empire.

New York: Harcourt, Brace, (1960) Print

Miller, T. (2019). Constantine changed calendar. Retrieved from http://www.lightbearerministries.org

Pastican, A. (2019). "How to bring a spirit of sabbath Into Your Daily Life Retrieved from http"//www.AlanPastian.com

Thomsen, E. (2003). What day is the sabbath and does it really matter? Sabbath Truth. Retrieved from https://www.sabbathtruth.com

About the Book

*T*he Savviness To Understanding and Embracing the Sabbath: A Journey From Sunday to Saturday is a book for everyone who desires to learn why embracing the Sabbath is still relevant for us today. It gives clear biblically based information on how to "Remember the Sabbath, to keep it holy." This book is an excellent guide on how to honor the Sabbath in such a spiritual, yet simplistic way that anyone can apply and live by.

There are many misconceptions regarding the truth about the Sabbath. Some say we should keep the Sabbath on Saturday, while others say it should be observed on Sunday. Some believe that only Jews should honor the Sabbath. Others believe the church (the body of Christ) is exempt from keeping it because of Jesus's finished work on the cross. Still others believe it is not necessary for us to keep the Sabbath at all today.

In this book, Lawrence and June clearly expound on the truths about the Sabbath, answer all those debated questions, and more. They have attended church on Sundays a combined total of thirty years. In this book, they share their unique journey of how the Lord led them to observe the seventh day and give a clear and concise outline that is thoroughly supported by the Bible.

About the Authors

Lawrence A. Saunders

*L*awrence A. Saunders is the Pastor of Word for Life Christian Church, which he planted in 2002 in Brooklyn, New York, where he was born and raised. Pastor Saunders is passionate about nurturing and discipling others. He loves preaching and teaching, as the Lord has gifted him with vast insight and revelation of the Word of God. Pastor Saunders is soundly educated, both spiritually and secularly. He has earned a Master's degree in Theology (Th.M.) and a Bachelor's degree in Public Administration. He was a lecturer of Public Speaking (Speech) at Medgar Everts College (CUNY) for four years.

Pastor Saunders' hobbies are coin collecting, fishing, and spending quality time with his son, Lawrence Saunders II. It is no coincidence that he enjoys fishing, as he is a "fisher of men." His personal motto is "I want more from God so I can do more for God."

June Tyson

Dr. June Tyson also comes to you from Brooklyn, New York. She is a Licensed Clinical Social Worker (LCSW-R) and a member of the Academy of Certified Social Workers (ACSW). She practices psychotherapy at Community Counseling and Mediation (CCM) in Brooklyn. She has a Master's degree in Social Work from Fordham University and a Ph.D in Human Services from Capella University. She is an adjunct professor in the Master's in Counseling Program and the Master's in Social Work Program at Liberty University, Indiana Wesleyan University, and Winthrop University.

She enjoys traveling as a missionary to Thailand, Mexico, and Haiti, and has taught English to students in these countries. Dr. Tyson is also part of a Global Heath Group with whom she travels, sharing Social Work techniques with doctors and nurses of various hospitals and universities in Nigeria.

Dr. Tyson has served the Christian community by teaching and living the Scriptures for more than thirty years. She is devoted to the things of the Lord and is led by the Holy Spirit in her professional and private life.

9 781545 678435